Pathfinder®Guides

G000297588

Peak District
Dark Peak

Walks

Compiled by
Dennis and Jan Kelsall

Text:	Dennis and Jan Kelsall
Photography:	Dennis and Jan Kelsall
Editorial:	Ark Creative (UK) Ltd
Design:	Ark Creative (UK) Ltd

ISBN 978-1-85458-494-6

While every care has been taken to ensure the accuracy of the route directions, the publishers cannot accept responsibility for errors or omissions, or for changes in details given. The countryside is not static: hedges and fences can be removed, field boundaries can alter, footpaths can be rerouted and changes in ownership can result in the closure or diversion of some concessionary paths. Also, paths that are easy and pleasant for walking in fine conditions may become slippery, muddy and difficult in wet weather, while stepping stones across rivers and streams may become impassable.

If you find an inaccuracy in either the text or maps, please write to Crimson Publishing at the address below.

First published in Great Britain 2009 by Crimson Publishing, a division of:

Crimson Business Ltd,
Westminster House, Kew Road, Richmond, Surrey, TW9 2ND

www.totalwalking.co.uk

Printed in Singapore. 1/09

A catalogue record for this book is available from the British library.

Front cover: Abandoned millstones below Stanage Edge
Previous page: On top of Whinstone Lee

Contents

Safety on the Hills;
Walkers and the Law;
Countryside Access Charter;
Useful Organisations;
Ordnance Survey Maps

Approximate walk times

 Up to 2½ hours   2½–3½ hours   4 hours and over

The walk times are provided as a guide only and are calculated using an average walking speed of 2½mph (4km/h), adding one minute for each 10m (33ft) of ascent, and then rounding the result to the nearest half hour.

WHITWORTH · Spring Mill Reservoir · Calderbrook · Summit · A672 · Scammonden Water · Outlane · HUDDERSFIELD

A6033 · A58 · Rishworth Moor 435 · Rishworth · Booth Wood · A640 · Golcar · A62 · Linthwaite

Wardle · Broadley · Healey · Smallbridge · LITTLEBOROUGH · Hollingworth Lake · Moselden Height · 472 · Slaithwaite · Holt Head · Linthwaite

ROCHDALE · Norden · Syke · A664 · Moss Moor · A640 · 466 · 453 · 500 · Blackmoorfoot Reservoir · Honley

MILNROW · Newhey · A640 · Castleshaw Moor 448 · 26 · Marsden · Butterley Reservoir · Meltham · Thick Hollins

SHAW · A627(M) · A6052 · Denshaw · Bleak Hey Nook · 17 · S · Pennine Way · Upperthong

ROYTON · Sholver · A672 · Delph · Diggle · 500 · 16 · Holme · House

MIDDLETON · OLDHAM · CHADDERTON · Lees · Uppermill · 15 · A635 · Black Hill 582 · A6024 · Saddleworth Moor · 523

CHADDERTON · A627 · Grasscroft 308 · Greenfield · 28 · 468 · Chew Reservoir · Salter Hebble

Blackley · Bardsley · MOSSLEY · 541 · 14

Cheetham Hill · Harpurhey · FAILSWORTH · Hurst · A635 · Buckton Vale · Millbrook · A670

MANCHESTER · ASHTON-UNDER-LYNE · STALYBRIDGE · Walkerwood Reservoir · Arnfield Brook · Totside Reservoir

DROYLSDEN · DUKINFIELD · Tintwistle · 21 · Bleaklow Hill 633

Gorton · Audenshaw · M67 · Hollingworth · B6105 · Pennine Way

Levenshulme · DENTON · Mottram in Longdendale · Hadfield · DOCTOR'S GATE · Snake Pass

Rusholme · HYDE · A560 · Gamesley · A6016 · GLOSSOP · A57

Withington · Burnage · Haughton Green · Broadbottom · Charlesworth · Chunal · Featherbed Top

Heaton Moor · Reddish · Bredbury · ROMILEY · Chisworth · 9 · 544 · Kinder Reservoir · Kinder Scout 636

STOCKPORT · Compstall · Pennine Bridleway · A624 · HIGH

CHEADLE · Offerton Green · MARPLE · Mellor 327 · 22 · field · Edale Cross

CHEADLE HULME · HAZEL GROVE · Hall · High Lane · NEW MILLS · Hayfield · Edale

BRAMHALL · Middlewood Sta · A6015 · Birch Vale · Chinley Head · Pennine Way · Barber Booth

Poynton · Higher Poynton · Disley · Newtown · Low Leighton · Furness Vale · 11 · Chinley

Handforth · Woodford · 408 Black Hill · Whaley Bridge · Chinley · Slackhall · Sparrowpit · Peak

WILMSLOW · Dean Row · Wood Lanes · Adlington · 13 · 410 · B5470 · Chapel-en-le-Frith · A623

ALDERLEY EDGE · A538 · Adlington Hall · Kettleshulme · Taxal · Fernilee · Combs · Dove Holes

Nether Alderley · Prestbury · Pott Shrigley · Fernilee Reservoir · Combs Reservoir · Peak Dale · NATIONAL

A34 · Tytherington · Kerridge · Rainow · Shining Tor · Errwood Reservoir · A5004 · Upper End · Wormhill · Wheston

Monk's Heath · Broken Cross · BOLLINGTON · Brookhouse · Lamaload Reservoir · A6 · 406

MACCLESFIELD · Hurdsfield · 397 · A537 · 559 · Goyt's Moss · BUXTON · Harpur Hill

Warren · Lyme Green · Langley · Macclesfield Forest · Cat and Fiddle · A54 · King Sterndale · A6 · A5270

Siddington · Sutton Lane · 506 · Axe Edge · Chelmorton

Eaton · North Rode · Wincle · Burntcliff Top · Hollinsclough · 422 · Longnor · Crowdecote

Brereton Heath · Bosley · Danebridge · Fawfieldhead · Newtown

Hulme Walfield · A54 · Key Green · Rushton Spencer · Heaton · 505 · Earl Sterndale

CONGLETON · Timbersbrook

Thornhill Edge HORBURY

Upper Hopton Kirkheaton Cowmes Whitley Lower Middlestown Netherton Crigglestone Walton Wintersett Ryhill Fitzwi

Fenay Bridge Lepton Grange Moor Flockton Midgley Chapelthorpe Woolley Edge Services South Hiendley HEMSWOR

Almondbury A642 A637 A636 West Bretton Woolley Notton ROYSTON Shafton Kinsley

Farnley Tyas Highburton Emley Moor Emley Darton Staincross Carlton Brierley Grime

Brockholes Shelley Skelmanthorpe Clayton West High Hoyland Kexbrough A637 BARNSLEY Cudworth A6195

Shepley New Mill Denby Dale A636 Cawthorne M1 A635 Gawber Priory Darfield

HOLMFIRTH Scholes Lane Head A635 Upper Denby Ingbirchworth Silkstone Dodworth WORSBROUGH Ardsley A633

Crow Edge Thurlstone A628 Hoylandswaine Silkstone Common Wombwell

Dunford Bridge PENISTONE Oxspring Thurgoland Wentworth Castle Birdwell Brampton

A628 Langsett **19** A629 Pilley Jump Elsecar

Upper Midhope MIDHOPE MOORS Midhopestones A616 Wortley A616 HOYLAND Wentworth Nether Haugh

HOWDEN MOORS STOCKSBRIDGE A6088 Deepcar High Green Thorpe Hesley Greasbrough

Bolsterstone **14** Ewden Village Chapeltown M1 A629

BRADFIELD MOORS High Bradfield Oughtibridge Grenoside A61 Ecclesfield A6135 Magna Tinsley

1 Low Bradfield Worrall Parson Cross Meadowhall A6102

3 **27** Dungworth Stannington P&R A61 Brinswort

6 SHEFFIELD A630

25 High Neb **12** Fulwood A625 A6102 A57

20 Hope **4** Bamford **8** Gleadless A61 A6135

18 Castleton **15** **23** Hathersage **2** Greenhill Waterthor

Bradwell Dore Beauchief Norton Ridgeway Highlane

Coplow Dale Abney Grindleford Totley Aston Eckington

Little Hucklow Grindlow Nether Padley Dronfield Woodhouse DRONFIELD Apperknowle Middle Handley

Foolow Eyam Eyam Hall Lydgate Holmesfield Unstone Green West Handley

Litton Stoney Middleton Froggatt Millthorpe Common Side Old Whittington STAVEL

Wardlow Calver Curbar Moorhall Barlow Newbold A6192 Woodth

Cressbrook A623 Baslow Robin Hood Cutthorpe CHESTERFIELD Brimington

Monsal Head A6020 Pilsley Chatsworth House Old Brampton A619 Calow A632

Ashford in the Water A619 Edensor Wadshell Holymoorside Walton Birdholme Hasland

Sheldon BAKEWELL Beeley Wingerworth A61 Sutton Scarsdale A617

Monyash Over Haddon A6 Haddon Hall Rowsley Spitewinter Tupton Alton Holmewood

Arbor Low Youlgrave Middleton Northwood Kelstedge Ashover North Wingfield

At-a-glance...

Walk	Page	Start	Nat. Grid Reference	Distance	Time	Height Gain
Black Moss and Butterley Reservoir	52	Marsden	SE 047118	6¼ miles (10.1km)	3 hrs	1,080ft (329m)
Bradfield Dale	12	Low Bradfield	SK 261920	2¾ miles (4.4km)	1½ hrs	570ft (174m)
Broomhead Reservoir	43	Bolsterstone	SK 270967	6 miles (9.7km)	3 hrs	1,000ft (305m)
Castleton and Mam Tor	55	Castleton	SK 149829	6¼ miles (10.1km)	3 hrs	1,325ft (404m)
Chinley Head	34	Chinley	SK 040827	5½ miles (8.9km)	3 hrs	1,250ft (381m)
Crowden and Millstone Rocks	64	Crowden	SK 072992	6½ miles (10.5km)	3½ hrs	1,550ft (472m)
Derwent Edge	86	Fairholmes National Park Centre	SK 172893	9 miles (14.5km)	4½ hrs	1,600ft (488m)
Digley Reservoir	49	Digley Reservoir	SE 109067	6¼ miles (10.1km)	3 hrs	1,075ft (328m)
Dovestone Edge	89	Binn Green	SE 017043	9¼ miles (14.9km)	4½ hrs	1,750ft (533m)
Edale and Jacob's Ladder	75	Edale	SK 123853	8 miles (12.9km)	4 hrs	1,690ft (515m)
Eldon Hole	24	Peak Forest	SK 113792	5 miles (8km)	2½ hrs	665ft (203m)
Hagg Side and Lockerbrook Heights	16	Fairholmes National Park Centre	SK 172893	4½ miles (7.2km)	2½ hrs	885ft (270m)
Hathersage	71	Hathersage	SK 231813	7¼ miles (11.7km)	3½ hrs	1,400ft (427m)
Higger Tor and Burbage Rocks	14	Upper Burbage Bridge	SK 260830	3¾ miles (6.0km)	2 hrs	720ft (219m)
Hope and Win Hill	18	Hope	SK 171835	4½ miles (7.2km)	2½ hrs	1,055ft (322m)
Langsett and Midhope Reservoirs	58	Langsett Reservoir	SE 210004	6½ miles (10.5km)	3 hrs	950ft (290m)
Lantern Pike	67	Hayfield	SK 036869	7¼ miles (11.7km)	3½ hrs	1,400ft (427m)
Lord's Seat	31	Barber Booth	SK 107847	5½ miles (8.9km)	3 hrs	1,150ft (351m)
Lose Hill	61	Edale	SK 123853	6 miles (9.7km)	3½ hrs	1,650ft (503m)
Lyme Park	40	Lyme Park	SJ 963823	6 miles (9.7km)	3 hrs	1,000ft (305m)
Marsden and Standedge	82	Marsden	SE 047118	8½ miles (13.7km)	4 hrs	1,300ft (396m)
Ramsden and Riding Wood Reservoirs	20	Ramsden Reservoir	SE 115056	4¾ miles (7.6km)	2½ hrs	970ft (296m)
Redmires Reservoirs	37	Wyming Brook	SK 268858	6 miles (9.7km)	3 hrs	850ft (259m)
Rowarth to Cown Edge	28	Rowarth near New Mills	SK 011892	5¾ miles (9.3km)	2½ hrs	840ft (256m)
Shatton Moor	46	Shatton	SK 203825	6 miles (9.7km)	3 hrs	1,200ft (366m)
Stanage Edge	26	Upper Burbage Bridge	SK 260830	5½ miles (8.9km)	2½ hrs	900ft (274m)
Whinstone Lee Tor and Cutthroat Bridge	22	Ashopton	SK 196864	4¾ miles (7.7km)	2½ hrs	1,025ft (312m)
Win Hill and Hope Cross	78	Ashopton	SK 202858	8¼ miles (13.3km)	4 hrs	1,590ft (485m)

Comments

The deep valleys above Marsden rise to the watershed of England. This ramble climbs onto the moors for a glimpse of Lancashire before finding a scenic return route past the reservoirs of the Wessenden Valley.

Despite the proximity of Sheffield, there is superb scenery and a fine sense of remoteness on this short walk.

Although barely a mile (1.6km) from the Stocksbridge steel works, the Broomhead valley is a world apart. Quiet woodlands by the lake contrast with airy hilltops on this pleasant round of the vale.

The narrow confines of Cave Dale contrast with the superb airy ridge of Mam Tor on this satisfying walk from Castleton, which should still leave time to visit one of the famous caves.

After an initial pull through old quarries above the town, the route wanders the margin between farm and moorland around Chinley Head.

Once a royal hunting forest, Longdendale now holds a string of reservoirs. This impressive walk onto the crags above reveals some of the finest views along its length.

Overlooking the Derwent and Ladybower reservoirs, Derwent Edge is punctuated with extraordinary rock formations, thoroughly justifying it as one of the Dark Peak's classic walks.

Tucked beneath the foreboding mass of Black Hill, the third highest in the Peak, the picturesque village of Holme is visited on this moorland promenade from Digley Reservoir.

The Dark Peak has no shortage of fine edge walks, but this one above the Dovestone reservoirs must rank among the most spectacular.

This ramble combines a dramatic ascent along Grindsbrook Clough with a superb edge walk past some of the exciting formations that dot the rim of the Kinder plateau.

The awesome, seemingly bottomless gash of Eldon Hole is listed as one of the *Wonders of the Peak*, and features on this walk into limestone country.

Hillside forest, lakeside and a short ridge highlight different aspects of the higher reaches of the Derwent Valley.

Literature, legend and landscape come together in this ramble from Hathersage. Associations with Charlotte Brontë, Jane Eyre, Robin Hood and Little John are all in this beautiful Derwent countryside.

Spectacular views and a fascinating prehistoric enclosure are highlights of this undemanding ramble.

Win Hill is one of the few Peakland tops rising to a distinguished peak and, although demanding a stiff climb, enjoys a fine prospect.

A variation to the classic walk around the popular Langsett Reservoir, which takes in the neighbouring water of Midhope and its surrounding forest.

Beginning from the attractive town of Hayfield, this circuit skirts the outlying flanks of the Kinder plateau to return over the former beacon hill of Lantern Pike and along the course of an old railway.

Lord's Seat provides the most dramatic ridge walk in the northern Peak, giving unrivalled prospects into Edale and across the limestone plateau to the south.

Gifted to G.H.B. Ward, one of the prime activists for access onto the moor, Lose Hill has assumed iconic status and marks the culmination of one of the finest ridge walks in the Peak.

Overlooking Manchester's suburbs from the edge of the National Park, the expanse of Lyme Park offers superb walking, extensive views and an opportunity to visit a grand mansion.

The head springs of the River Tame and the River Colne almost touch on Standedge, from which there are superb views along the valleys both east and west.

This walk wanders the upper reaches of the Holme Valley, which provided many of the countryside settings for the ever-popular *Last of the Summer Wine*.

Once a training ground for the Sheffield Pals regiment, the lonely Redmires moors are now popular with walkers escaping the busyness of the nearby city.

The western fringes of the Dark Peak overlook the Cheshire plain, and although the hills are not high, they offer impressive views across the landscape.

Following lanes and old tracks onto Shatton Moor, this simple ramble reveals a different perspective over the Hope Valley and takes in the site of a Roman fort.

Stanage Edge is one of the finest escarpments of the north-eastern moors. Easily attained from Upper Burbage it offers a grand high-level walk.

A roundabout route through a woodland nature reserve and across the moors offers a leisurely approach to the spectacular views of Derwent Edge.

The long, broad tail of Win Hill reveals a changing perspective across the valleys of the Ashop and the Noe, which fall on either side. The walk returns beside the long western arm of the Ladybower Reservoir.

Introduction to the Peak District

The area known as the Peak encompasses the southern extremity of the Pennine uplift, the longest contiguous range of hills in the country, which runs from the Scottish borders all the way to the Midland plains. Much of the Peak falls within Derbyshire, but the hills over-spill into the counties of Yorkshire, Staffordshire, Cheshire and Greater Manchester too. Despite a relatively compact size, barely 40 miles (64km) from top to bottom and only 20 miles (32km) wide, it embodies vividly contrasting landscapes, their disparate characters springing from the bedrock upon which they lie. The highest land is to be found in the north and is footed on gritstone, a hard impermeable sandstone that weathers almost to black. It gives rise to vast rolling moors abruptly bounded by dark dramatically weatherworn cliffs known as 'edges'. Farther south, the gritstone runs out in two peripheral horns that embrace a lower, grassy limestone plateau, neatly partitioned by miles of drystone walls and riven by pretty dales and deep gorges, which grace the area with much of its beauty.

The word 'peak' might conjure an image of dramatic pinnacles and lofty heights, perhaps attained only after the effort of a scramble. But here you will find few craggy summits or prodigious heights, the greatest elevation of 2,088 feet (636m) being barely distinguishable amid an unrelieved wilderness on the Kinder plateau. 'Peak' in fact derives from the Old English word paec, meaning merely a hill, and the Anglo-Saxon peoples who settled here after the Romans abandoned Britain in the 5th century became known as the Pecsætna or Peak Dwellers. The name stuck and today describes one of the most popular regions for outdoor activity in the country.

The National Park

Despite the lack of 'peaks', this is grand walking country and was appreciated as such long before the National Park came into existence. By the close of the 19th century, industrial expansion was pushing at the edge of the moors and many factory workers looked to the clear, open spaces on their doorstep for recreation; a chance to escape the crowding, noise and dirt of their workaday lives. However, most of the land was private, preserved as grouse moors, sheep runs or water catchment for the numerous reservoirs being built in the higher valleys. Many viewed this blanket prohibition as a deep injustice and braved the often-aggressive gamekeepers to practise the 'gentle art of trespass'. Ramblers' groups and footpath preservation societies achieved some success in opening Rights of Way, yet the Kinder Trespass in 1932 was a milestone. Although neither the first nor the last mass trespass, it became iconic, partly because of its scale, some 500 people took to the moor, but also for the harshness of punishment meted out to the handful of ringleaders arrested. This turned the tide of public sympathy and developed a will to change the law, which eventually led to the enactment of the National Park and Access to the Countryside Act in 1949 and subsequently, the *Countryside and Rights of Way Act in 2000.*

Above Ashway Rocks

The Peak District National Park was created in 1951 as a direct result of the 1949 Act, the first of its kind in Britain. In relation to its size, 555 square miles (1,437km²), it is the second most visited in the country, not surprising since roughly half of England's population is calculated to live within a couple of hours' drive. Yet, despite this proximity to so many people, the park has only one settlement, Bakewell, that can be called a town, and huge tracts of the Peak remain totally unspoiled. Its most famous beauty spots are justifiably popular and are best avoided on a summer's weekend. But with 124 square miles (321km²) of open access land and 1,867 miles (3,005km) of designated Rights of Way, it is possible even on the busiest bank holiday to spend a day on the hills or in the remoter valleys and hardly see a soul.

The Dark Peak

The geological boundary between the grit and limestone is abrupt and describes an arc that has Castleton at its most northerly point. The northern gritstone is so named because its hardness made it an ideal material for use as stones for grist mills, and in places such as Stanage, you can come across great rock cheeses, ready cut and shaped but, for some reason, never removed from the quarries. Indeed, so important was the millstone to the area that the Peak District National Park has adopted it as its emblem. But the character of the stone varies subtly from place to place and countless quarries like those at Cracken Edge and above Crowden exploited the rock for many different purposes. Indeed, almost anywhere you might stumble on a small quarry used to supply stone for local building, not least for the numerous reservoirs that fill the valleys cleaving its flanks.

Although the high, inhospitable moorlands provided a check on industrial growth into the Peak, the prodigious torrents falling from the heights, made more productive by the construction of small reservoirs, were exploited to power the first factory mills. As the conurbations surrounding Manchester, Sheffield and Derby grew, so did their need for water. The city fathers commissioned ever-larger dams, a process that continued through the 20th century with Dovestones, completed in 1967, being among the more recent. Having no natural lakes, these man-made bodies of water have had a huge impact upon the landscape of the Peak. Lonely valleys and cloughs have been lost together with many hilltop farms and, in the case of Ladybower, a couple of villages too. But the flood has created a different scenery not necessary less pleasing and often enhanced by the planting of woodland and forest around the shores such as at Langsett, Derwent and Broomhead. Nature has been quick to adapt to the changing conditions and birdlife in particular has exploited many of the opportunities created.

For much of their length, the Pennines have acted as a natural barrier between east and west. The Peak was no exception and travel has never been easy along the relatively small number of steep and often boggy packhorse trails that crossed the high moors. Even today, there are not many roads and these are susceptible to closure during winter storms. But, as the industrial age dawned, engineers dared, in the words of one 1960s TV series 'to boldly go where no man has gone before'. Amazingly, canals were pushed across, racked up along the valleys on lock staircases with two, including the Huddersfield Narrow Canal, attaining their summit in tunnels beneath the moors. Imposing viaducts and more tunnels later brought the railways, not in themselves significantly changing the landscape, but bringing in people and opening markets for quarries and coal. Trains still run through Marsden and along the Edale Valley, while the disused trackbed through Longdendale now offers easy walking (and cycling) amid impressive scenery.

While there may be few peaks, the high escarpments that bound the upland plateaux and known locally as 'edges' are equally dramatic features of this northern terrain. They rise as weather-worn cliffs above deep valleys and cloughs and many are the special haunt of rock climbers who, like the ramblers in the early years of the 20th century, braved the wrath of gamekeepers to follow their sport on the forbidden crags. Once attained, edges such as Stanage, Dovestone, Derwent and Standedge offer miles of splendid walking.

The over-riding character of the Dark Peak, however, is that of its high undulating moor. It often appears a true wilderness, an all but featureless and seemingly limitless expanse of peat, tussock and heather. Yet even this can be breathtaking as in late summer the heath assumes a regal cloak of purple. Much is open access land, but definite paths are few and far between and even those can become difficult to follow in bad weather. Although at one time wooded, the cover has long since gone, stripped bare by prehistoric overgrazing and a subsequent cooler, wetter climate. Sparse grasses, spike rush, cotton grass, heathers and bilberry are the plants to be found here, while the poorly drained tops are often covered by peat bog.

Itinerant sheep appear totally ignorant of their solitude and, apart from the odd secretive vole scurrying through the grass or perhaps a fleet-footed hare, the only other life to be seen are the birds. Red grouse are common, indeed much of the heather moorland is specifically managed for their benefit, but come the 'Glorious Twelfth', it is payback time. Among the birds of prey you might spot are the hen harrier, goshawk, merlin and even peregrine falcon, while winchat, ring ouzel, dunlin and golden plover are also about.

The walks
Many of the routes are focussed upon reservoirs, valleys and the edges of the moors, where there are obvious landmarks to guide the way. Elsewhere, the vast, featureless spaces may appear intimidating to the inexperienced, but most of the described walks follow discernible paths, which, in fine weather, should present no great difficulty to the sensible novice. *But, be aware that conditions on the tops can be markedly different from those in the valleys and can very rapidly deteriorate. Adequate clothing and provisions and the ability to navigate using map and compass are necessary. It is easy to become disoriented in mist and, in this empty terrain, a GPS receiver can be a useful additional tool to pinpoint your position.* The longer moorland walks do present a challenge and newcomers to rambling would be advised to develop their experience on the less demanding routes first.

In an area where there is so much worthy of exploration, the difficulty is not in what to include, but rather what to leave out. This collection has been chosen to explore the many different aspects of the countryside and sometimes include or lie close to another attraction.

The Park Authority does an excellent job in maintaining paths, stiles and gates and, in recent years, the water authorities have opened many trails around their reservoirs and surrounding forests. Together with canal towpaths, former railway lines, old tracks and quiet lanes, they offer endless possibilities for superb walking. There is an on-going policy to replace stiles with gates in popular areas, but you can expect to encounter at least some stiles and squeeze gaps on every walk. In most places, well-behaved dogs are welcome and ought to be kept on leads near livestock, in farmyard areas and while passing through nature reserves. They should also be restrained during the spring nesting season upon the moor and note also that, in some open access areas, dogs are not permitted other than on Rights of Way.

This book includes a list of waypoints alongside the description of the walk, so that you can enjoy the full benefits of gps should you wish to. For more information on using your gps, read the *Pathfinder® Guide GPS for Walkers*, by gps teacher and navigation trainer, Clive Thomas (ISBN 978-0-7117-4445-5). For essential information on map reading and basic navigation, read the *Pathfinder® Guide Map Reading Skills* by outdoor writer, Terry Marsh (ISBN 978-0-7117-4978-8). Both titles are available in bookshops or can be ordered online at www.totalwalking.co.uk

Bradfield Dale

		GPS waypoints
Start	Low Bradfield	SK 261 920
Distance	2¾ miles (4.4km)	Ⓐ SK 262 925
Height gain	570 feet (174m)	Ⓑ SK 268 924
Approximate time	1½ hours	Ⓒ SK 264 916
Parking	Car park by recreation ground	Ⓓ SK 254 917
Route terrain	Field and woodland paths and lanes	
Ordnance Survey maps	Landranger 110 (Sheffield & Huddersfield), Explorer OL1 (The Peak District – Dark Peak area)	

Barely a stone's throw from Sheffield, the Loxley Valley is a gateway to open countryside. This ramble between the attractive settlements of Low and High Bradfield swaps woodland paths for hillside views, and an early Norman fort, village pub and ancient church are features along the way.

Emerging from the car park entrance, double back right along a walled path to the river. Instead of crossing, continue upstream to a second bridge, from which a stepped path rises steeply to a gap beside a redundant stile in the upper wall. The path continues opposite to meet a lane at the top. Follow it left beside the Agden Reservoir, one of four in the area that help supply Sheffield's needs. Rounding

a bend, look for a path leaving on the right about 300 yds along Ⓐ.

Signed to Bailey Hill, it climbs sharply at the edge of a forest plantation and eventually reaches a junction of paths. The onward way lies through a squeeze stile on the right, but first wander ahead to Bailey Hill, the site of a Norman motte-and-bailey castle. Although overgrown with trees, the earth ramparts and ditches remain a formidable sight, dominated by a towering conical mound on which stood the donjon or keep. Return to the stile and pass beside the extension cemetery to the old graveyard surrounding Bradfield's church.

St Nicholas's is a fine building, surprisingly large and imposing for such a small village and was endowed and staffed by monks of the former priory at Ecclesfield, a

Bailey Hill

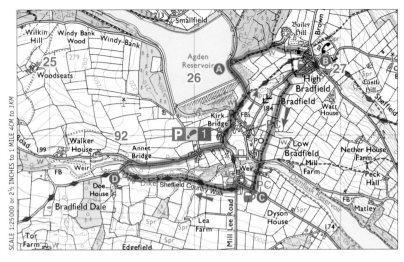

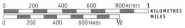

once remote place that has now become engulfed within the suburbs of Sheffield. Its superb Perpendicular architecture dates from the 15th century, although the tower remains from an earlier building. Inside is a Celtic cross, which was placed there in 1886. The curious Gothic structure at the north-eastern corner of the churchyard is the Watch House, built in 1745 for a guard employed to deter body-snatchers from plundering the graves.

Leave over a stile behind the Watch House and follow the street round past the church gates and through the village. The area was the centre of a prosperous domestic knitting industry, the three storey houses built to accommodate knitting frames in the well-windowed upper rooms. Go beyond the end of Towngate to the **Old Horns Inn** Ⓑ. Turn beside it into Woodfall Lane, dropping steeply for 250 yds to a bend where a waymarked wall stile broaches the left wall. Marked to Low Bradfield, a path skirts the top edge of a field. Crossing another stile and initially with a wall on your left, head downhill through successive

fields. Over a final stile, negotiate awkward steps to the lane below. Cross to a track almost opposite and follow it over a bridge and past a junction to meet a second lane Ⓒ.

Go right to **The Plough** and then turn left, walking a few steps up the hill before leaving along a walled track on the right. Across the valley is a view back to Bradfield church, while to the north on the skyline above the woodland cloaking the Agden Valley are the rocks of Hurkling Edge. Beyond cottages, where the track finishes, mount a stile and keep on at the top edge of grazing above Dale Dike. The tranquil stream emanates from the Dale Dike Reservoir, built in 1864. Tragically, just after completion, the dam wall failed, unleashing a raging torrent that devastated Low Bradfield. The flood wreaked havoc along the valley to the centre of Sheffield and almost 300 people lost their lives while thousands were left homeless.

Towards the far side of the second field, angle down to a stile out to a narrow lane Ⓓ. Cross Annet Bridge and climb to a junction above, going right again towards Low Bradfield. Dropping into the village, walk past a junction and then shortly swing left along The Sands back to the car park. ●

Higger Tor and Burbage Rocks

		GPS waypoints	
Start	Upper Burbage Bridge	🖉 SK 260 830	
Distance	3¾ miles (6km)	Ⓐ SK 256 820	
Height gain	720 feet (219m)	Ⓑ SK 258 815	
Approximate time	2 hours	Ⓒ SK 262 805	
Parking	Car park west of bridge	Ⓓ SK 270 815	
Route terrain	Occasionally bouldery, but clear moorland paths		
Ordnance Survey maps	Landranger 110 (Sheffield & Huddersfield), Explorer OL1 (The Peak District – Dark Peak area)		

Although short and undemanding, this circuit around the head of Burbage Brook lacks for nothing in stunning scenery. The route climbs over the spectacular viewpoint of Higger Tor to a second dramatic outcrop, long held to be a prehistoric fort. The return follows a superb edge overlooking the eastern side of the valley.

🖉 Begin from the small car park to the west of Upper Burbage Bridge, from which two paths are signed through a small gate. The higher one contours the slope of Fiddler's Elbow above the valley, undulating towards your first objective, the flat-topped hill of Higger Tor Ⓐ.

From Higger Tor to the head of the Burbage Valley

Bouldery on top and flanked by rocky buttresses, the platform offers a panorama across the Derwent Valley and the deep rift cradling Burbage Brook.

Descend from the southern tip to a clear path across Hathersage Moor, which leads onto the promontory of Carl Wark Ⓑ. Projecting above the valley it is a natural citadel secured by a high boulder and earth rampart that incorporates a defended gateway below the south-eastern corner. Nearby burial mounds, cairns and dwelling platforms indicate settlement since the Bronze Age, but the true purpose of Carl Wark remains a mystery. Neighbouring forts on Mam Tor and at Navio suggest a military purpose, but today's historians argue that Higger Tor would then have been the more logical site. Limited excavations in 1950 failed to reveal decisive evidence and modern thinking favours a protective retreat for livestock and people in times of trouble.

Leave the enclosure at the far end of the wall, from which the ongoing path falls away across a bouldery slope. After breasting another lower outcrop, the path drops to the road beside Burbage Bridge. Crossing the bridge, follow the road up to a small car park ●.

For an undemanding return, take the broad track from the back of the car park, which contours the valley side below the cliffs of Burbage Rocks. Known as the Duke's Drive, it led up to the grouse moors from the Duke of Rutland's shooting retreat, Longshaw Lodge, which is now owned by the National Trust.

However, the more interesting route follows a path along the top of the escarpment and is signposted to the right from beside the car park entrance. Through a small gate onto the open moor, head up the slope towards the ridge. Keep right where the path shortly forks, later passing a stone block, abandoned after it cracked while being fashioned into a water trough.

The path gains the top of the scar above an old quarry, suddenly revealing an impressive view across the valley, and continues along the rim, gently rising to the high point directly opposite Carl Wark. From here, its position appears even more impregnable, despite its subordination to Higger Tor. The cliffs then run out and the way descends, curving left to a junction by a waymark and cairn ●.

Keep ahead, losing height to ford a stream before climbing once more to the continuing line of cliffs. The airy walk finally comes to an end as both path and lower track meet the lane beside Upper Burbage Bridge. ●

Hagg Side and Lockerbrook Heights

Hagg Side and Lockerbrook Heights

		GPS waypoints
Start	Fairholmes National Park Centre	 SK 172 893
Distance	4½ miles (7.2km)	Ⓐ SK 180 885
Height gain	885 feet (270m)	Ⓑ SK 170 885
Approximate time	2½ hours	Ⓒ SK 164 891
Parking	At start – Pay and Display	Ⓓ SK 166 910
Route terrain	Forest tracks	Ⓔ SK 170 897
Ordnance Survey maps	Landranger 110 (Sheffield & Huddersfield), Explorer OL1 (The Peak District – Dark Peak area)	

After an initial stretch beside Ladybower, the route climbs the steep, forested flanks of Hagg Side to swing north across Lockerbrook Heights. There are views across Ashop, Edale and into the upper Derwent before dropping to an easy finish beside the Derwent reservoir and dam.

Despite the sense of natural beauty pervading the upper Derwent Valley, the scenescape is almost entirely due to man. The three vast lakes of Howden, Derwent and Ladybower were created as reservoirs to supply growing industrial cities and the conifer forests were planted for timber and to purify the water draining the catchment. Together with the open moorland of the upper slopes, the area annually attracts over two million visitors who explore the many

The Derwent Dam

pathways and tracks on foot or by bike, fish the lakes or simply admire the view. The woodlands around the visitor centre attract many small birds and in the clearings of the wider forest you might spot a goshawk hunting for a meal. Now becoming more common, these are bold hunters and will pursue other birds into the tree cover or take small mammals such as squirrels and rabbits.

From the **Fairholmes Visitor Centre**, go back to the road. Turn left and walk for ¼ mile to a roadside parking area from which you will find a path signed to the Bridge End car park. Dropping through the woodland fringe below the road, it undulates easily above the lake. Shortly after leaving the trees by a small, stone water-board building, bear right back to the road and cross to the Bridge End car park opposite Ⓐ.

A broad loggers' track leaves beside it, climbing steeply into the plantation above. After some ½ mile, bear right at a fork along a lesser track, which rises more easily and shortly ends at a couple of gates and stiles **B**. Cross and go right along an open track, once the old pack road across the moors to Glossop and which is signed to Alport Bridge. The Hagg Side plantation precludes a view to the lake far below, but over to the left the eye is drawn across the Ashop Valley to the bleak eastern promontory of the Kinder plateau. Farther back, overlooking Edale is the long ridge running from Lose Hill past the precipice of Back Tor to the distant Iron Age fortress of Mam Tor. Keep going above the edge of the forest, eventually crossing a stile beside a gate.

Drop to a meeting of tracks beyond **C**, and follow that to the right, heading almost due north. It carries on gradually downward beside the forest, eventually crossing Locker Brook to reach Lockerbrook Farm, now operating as an outdoors activity centre. Remain on the rising track through a gate beyond the farm, which soon crests to a long descent back in the trees. Ignore the track later signed off to Fairholmes, continuing ever more steeply down until you ultimately reach the road at the foot of Ouzelden Clough **D**.

Follow the lakeside road to the right, eventually passing the Derwent Dam, where the western tower houses a small museum dedicated to RAF 617 Squadron. The pilots used the valley during the spring of 1943 while training for a daring attack upon the Möhne and Eder dams in the industrial heartland of Nazi Germany. There is also a memorial to a faithful sheepdog, 'Tip', who guarded the body of her master for 15 weeks after he died on the Howden moors during the winter of 1953–54.

A few yards beyond, look for a path signed off to Fairholmes **E**, which drops into trees above the reservoir outflow. Keep right at a fork and walk out to another lane. Go left and almost immediately right on a path that leads back to the visitor centre and car park. ●

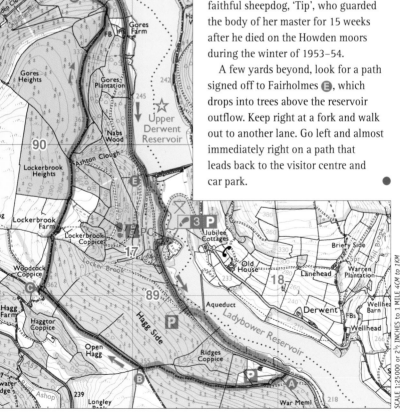

Hope and Win Hill

		GPS waypoints
Start	Hope	🖉 SK 171 835
Distance	4½ miles (7.2km)	Ⓐ SK 171 838
Height gain	1,055 feet (322m)	Ⓑ SK 186 850
Approximate time	2½ hours	Ⓒ SK 192 850
Parking	Car park on main street – Pay and Display	Ⓓ SK 186 839
		Ⓔ SK 179 837
Route terrain	Field and moorland paths	
Ordnance Survey maps	Landranger 110 (Sheffield & Huddersfield), Explorer OL1 (The Peak District – Dark Peak area)	

Although short, this walk involves a strenuous ascent of Win Hill, but the effort expended is amply rewarded with a panoramic view from the top. The enjoyable return through woodland, heath and field ends along the banks of the River Noe in the Hope Valley.

🖉 Go right out of the car park along the main street to the church and turn left into Edale Road. Stride up the lane for ¼ mile to a fork just after the school Ⓐ. Bear right along Bowden Lane signed to Hope Cemetery, the way dropping over the River Noe at Killhill Bridge. Climbing beyond, pass beneath a railway bridge and then turn right, the lane becoming a farm track as it curves away from the woodland bordering the line. Carry on up the hill to Twitchill Farm, walking through the yard to a gate at the top.

A path rises steeply ahead up the fellside to another gate, continuing in the next field to a stile at the top corner. A clear path carries on steadily upwards through the gorse, heather and bracken of open moorland, but pause occasionally to appreciate the views opening behind as you gain height. Beyond a broken wall, the gradient eases and the distinctive rocky peak of Win Hill now appears ahead. The main path makes straight for it, passing through a kissing-gate to join another path for the

final stretch to the summit Ⓑ.

To the north, the ground falls abruptly to the Ladybower Reservoir and above the timber-clad slopes of the Derwent Valley is the impressive line of Derwent Edge. Farther west is the brooding mass of Kinder Scout, while more immediately, across the head of the Hope Valley is Lose Hill, whose long ridge stretches back to Mam Tor and Lord's Seat.

The path follows the short but splendidly ragged ridge, the high point of the walk in more ways than one. From the end it falls quickly to a gate and, where the path forks beyond, take the left branch, into the Winhill Plantation. Continue down through the trees, in a little while reaching a junction of paths in front of a wall and fence Ⓒ.

To the right the way is signed to Thornhill and contours beside a wall around the hill. After some ¼ mile, bear right at a junction through a gap in the wall. A lesser but still distinct path signed to Aston rises over a shoulder of

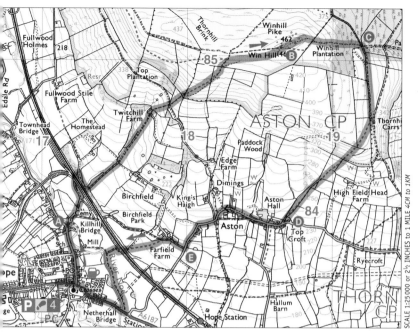

bilberry and heather moor before losing height to a wall stile. Carry on down the hill, passing through a gate in the corner to continue along a narrow enclosure. Over a stile at the bottom follow a contained path, which leads onto a narrow lane **D**.

Turn right and keep with the main lane for a little over ¹/₂ mile past the old

The trig point on Winhill Pike

hall and scattered farms and cottages that comprise the hamlet of Aston. Despite the tarmac, the walking here is a delight, for the way drops below occasional wooded banks, the rocks oozing moisture and dripping with mosses and fern. Carry on until you reach a track off right to Farfield Farm **E**.

Follow it as far as the farmhouse and there bear off left on a track signed to the camping field that drops to a gate beside a barn. Leave through a small kissing-gate on the left and head away, initially beside the right-hand hedge and continuing beyond its end to a gate at the bottom of the field. Entering woodland bordering a railway embankment, go right and then left beneath a bridge into the field on the other side. Strike across to meet the bank of the River Noe and walk downstream alongside it to a bridge. Climb out to the main road and follow it across the river back into Hope.

Ramsden and Riding Wood Reservoirs

		GPS waypoints
Start	Ramsden Reservoir	
Distance	4¾ miles (7.6km)	✐ SE 115 056
Height gain	970 feet (296m)	Ⓐ SE 117 055
		Ⓑ SE 129 049
Approximate time	2½ hours	Ⓒ SE 119 053
Parking	Car park at start	Ⓓ SE 111 050
		Ⓔ SE 109 059
Route terrain	Lane, tracks and rough but generally clear moorland paths *Note: The Riding Wood Dam is closed until spring 2010*	
Ordnance Survey maps	Landranger 110 (Sheffield & Huddersfield), Explorer OL1 (The Peak District – Dark Peak area)	

The River Holme drains the steep eastern flank of Black Hill, rising to 1,909 feet (582m, the third highest point in the Peak). The reservoirs and woodland of its upper reaches contrast with the bleaker scenery of the surrounding moors and this exploration of the Ramsden Valley takes in Holme, where the Fleece Inn provides a convenient lunchtime stop.

✐ A track leaves the lane beside the entrance to the Ramsden car park, climbing past a picnic area and stand of conifers. As it swings right at the top, go over the stile facing you Ⓐ. Bear left to a break in a stone wall and continue on a clear trod across the sloping fields. Keep going as the way becomes enclosed as a walled track, in a little while passing above Moss Edge Farm.

Through a gate a little farther on, the more obvious track curves right. However, take the rougher track ahead, passing through a broken gateway. A narrower path contours the hillside above Dobb Dike, eventually bending round to ford the stream towards its head. Walk away, choosing the obliquely rising path that leads out to a wide lane, White Gate Road. Turn right, passing Upper White Gate Farm and shortly

reaching a junction of tracks by the corner of Copthurst Moor Plantation Ⓑ.

Turn off sharp right along a stony track, Ramsden Road, the rising heather on the left soon giving way to the pine wood of Crossley's Plantation. Beyond there, the track falls in gentle descent, revealing a splendid view along the Holme Valley.

Eight miles (12.9km) distant is the Emley Moor transmitter mast, which, at 1,084 feet (330m), is the tallest free-standing structure in the country and transmits digital and (until 2011) analogue TV signals to some four million homes in Yorkshire. Brought on air in 1971, the elegant concrete tower is a Grade 2 listed building and replaced an earlier mast blown down in a storm. Farther left is the Jubilee Tower on Castle Hill, built in 1898 to commemorate 60

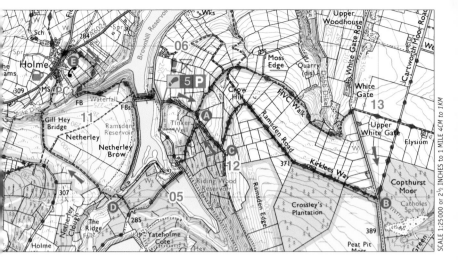

SCALE 1:25000 or 2½ INCHES to 1 MILE 4CM to 1KM

```
0    200   400   600   800 METRES   1
                                    KILOMETRES
                                    MILES
0    200   400   600 YARDS   ½
```

years of Queen Victoria's reign.

Keep with the main track as it later swings left.

Reaching a junction , go right, dropping to a sharp bend. The path to the right takes you straight back to the Ramsden car park. The walk, however, continues left down into the forest to meet a lane opposite a cottage above the head of the Ramsden Reservoir. Go left and follow it over the dam of the Riding Wood Reservoir (* see Note). After ¼ mile at a left bend, look out for a stile over the wall on the right. Drop beside a wall, passing through a gap at the bottom, beyond which the path falls left to a bridge at the base of Netherley Clough.

Climb away over a stile, soon encountering a stream . Turn off immediately before it on a path rising back across the hillside and then turning straight up. The gradient shortly eases and the path continues across rough sheep pasture, eventually reaching a stile. Keep ahead with a broken wall on your left. Ultimately the path drops into Rake Dike. Climbing away more easily, the onward path heads toward the cottages of Holme. Leave the field through the garden of a white house and walk out to the road opposite the **Fleece Inn**. Turn right through the village.

Beyond the Sunday school, look for a path signed off on the right , which drops past the appropriately named Underhill, the first earth-sheltered home to be built in Britain by the architect Arthur Quarmby in the late 1970s. Continue downfield, slipping through a gate part-way along onto a contained path. Over stiles at the bottom, turn right across the slope of the hill, descending back into Rake Dike to a bridge overlooking a small waterfall. The ongoing path climbs back above the head of the Brownhill Reservoir before dropping to the Ramsden Dam. Cross and walk up to the lane above, where the Ramsden car park lies just to the right.   ●

Netherley Clough

Whinstone Lee Tor and Cutthroat Bridge

		GPS waypoints
Start	Ashopton – lay-by beside A57	⬚ SK 196 864
Distance	4¾ miles (7.7km)	Ⓐ SK 198 865
Height gain	1,025 feet (312m)	Ⓑ SK 220 878
Approximate time	2½ hours	Ⓒ SK 203 880
Parking	Lay-by beside A57 at the start	Ⓓ SK 197 874
Route terrain	Generally good moorland paths, but *take care in mist*	
Ordnance Survey maps	Landranger 110 (Sheffield & Huddersfield), Explorer OL1 (The Peak District – Dark Peak area)	

Tackled from Derwent, the Derwent Edge demands a strenuous climb. But this roundabout route above Ladybower Brook and the moor behind the scarp adopts a more leisurely approach. Stunning views accompany the return past the southern-most of the outcrops, for which the edge is famous.

This enjoyable walk revels in splendid scenery and passes through one of the Peak District's few remaining oak woods. This was once the predominant vegetation of the northern Peak and in the sloping shelter of the valley, there is a rich variety of plant life, including mosses, lichens and ferns. Limestone erupts just to the south, but here the hills are gritstone, their exposed tops cloaked in peat and heather moor that is home to red grouse. The lack of cover also encourages predators such as peregrine and merlin, which hover motionless in the wind before swooping down upon their prey. And, if your luck is really in, you might also see a mountain hare.

⬚ From the parking area, walk towards the viaduct spanning the northern arm of the Ladybower Reservoir. Just before, cross to a rising tarmac drive and follow it around a sharp bend. Through a gate continue to the end, where a path is signed to Cutthroat Bridge through a small gate ahead Ⓐ.

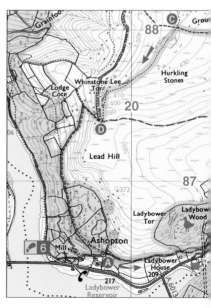

Contouring the bracken-clad hillside, there is a fine view to the Ladybower Dam before passing into woodland. Meeting a track rising from the **Ladybower Inn**, follow it up the hill and through a gate into the Ladybower Woods Nature Reserve. When the track splits, branch right, shortly fording a small brook cascading down the hill. Carry on to another fork above Cutthroat Bridge.

Keep ahead, clambering down to negotiate a stream. The path then wanders easily across the hillside eventually leading to a ladder-stile. Just beyond, is an ancient milestone, marking the old road to Sheffield.

Passing through a field-gate **B**, immediately turn left on a track rising beside a wall and signed to Derwent via Derwent Edge. Scale a stile by a second gate higher up and continue across the open heather moor. After dipping to re-cross the stream encountered earlier the path rises to a fork by a T-shaped grouse butt. Bear left and carry on up

Dropping below Lead Hill

the hill, later passing a lone standing stone beside the path before you finally broach the ridge to encounter a crossing path **C**.

The onward route lies to the left, but it is worth first wandering a little way along the path ahead for the view into the upper Derwent Valley and along the edge past the Wheel Stones to White Tor. Heading south from the junction, the path gradually loses height past the Hurkling Stones and Whinstone Lee Tor. After a while you reach another crossing of paths **D** beside a small promontory overlooking the foot of the lake, a further opportunity to dally while enjoying the superb vista.

The way down lies along the footpath to the right, not the bridleway leaving sharp right. It falls steeply through a rocky cleft before sweeping left across a bracken slope to then run beside a wall. The dramatic views are eventually lost as the path encounters plantation, swapping the far-reaching panorama for more intimate scenes amongst the rich greens and browns of the forest. Ultimately passing through a gate, you are returned to the head of the track up which the walk began **A**. Follow it back to the main road. ●

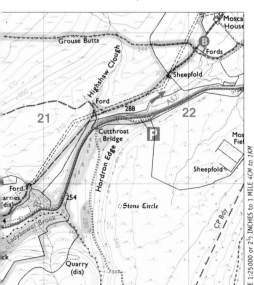

Eldon Hole

		GPS waypoints
Start	Peak Forest	✎ SK 113 792
Distance	5 miles (8km)	Ⓐ SK 114 797
Height gain	665 feet (203m)	Ⓑ SK 117 804
Approximate time	2½ hours	Ⓒ SK 116 808
Parking	Street parking in village	Ⓓ SK 122 813
Route terrain	Upland pastures, generally clear tracks and paths	Ⓔ SK 135 813
		Ⓕ SK 132 805
Ordnance Survey maps	Landrangers 110 (Sheffield & Huddersfield) and 119 (Buxton & Matlock), Explorers OL1 (The Peak District – Dark Peak area) and OL24 (The Peak District – White Peak area)	

In the 17th century, Eldon Hole was described in Latin verse by Thomas Hobbs as one of the 'Great Marvels of the Peak'. Time has done nothing to diminish the fascination of this dramatic 180 feet (55m) deep pothole, which features on this pleasant ramble from the nearby village of Peak Forest.

✎ Leave the main road crossroads at the centre of the village opposite the church along Church Lane, which leads to the neighbouring hamlet of Old Dam. At the junction, bear left, walking for another 150 yds before turning off into Eldon Lane Ⓐ.

Beyond Sweet Knoll Farm, the lane degrades to a track, rising through a gate and stile onto access land. Walk up 30 yds to the top of the intake Ⓑ and, leaving the ongoing bridleway, swing left with the wall, accompanying it towards a strip of woodland. The trees stand along an outcropping vein of lead ore, whose course, pockmarked with the scars of innumerable small pits and spoil heaps, can be traced in a shallow curve across the open hillside. Continue through a gate by the trees, now making for the dark gash of Eldon Hole Ⓒ.

Close to, Eldon Hole reveals itself as an awesome gape penetrating the earth, which inspired legends of supernatural mystery. The seemingly bottomless pit suggested a gateway to a subterranean labyrinth inhabited by elves and goblins that could bring both good and bad luck. Local folk gave the pot a wide berth and it was not until 1780 that the first recorded descent took place. However, the unfortunate explorer returned demented and expired within days of his terrifying ordeal at the end of a rope. Stories of a goose being put in and reappearing days later from the caves at Castleton suggested Eldon Hole's connection to a network of caverns, but another century passed before John Tym and Rooke Pennington of Castleton discovered the cave system at its foot.

Heading roughly south east, make your way across the shoulder of open grazing above the walled line of old workings to regain the bridleway abandoned earlier. Follow it left over the crest of the hill, continuing through

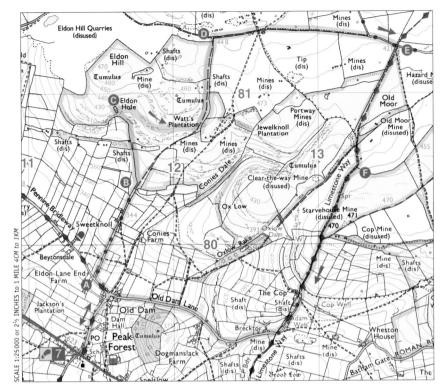

SCALE 1:25000 or 2½ INCHES to 1 MILE 4CM to 1KM

a gate along an enclosed section to meet a broad, walled track **D**.

Follow the drove to the right, passing more evidence of old lead workings in the tussock-veiled craters of the Slitherstone Mines. The prominent hill to the north that later comes into view is Mam Tor, notorious for an ongoing landslip that began some 4,000 years ago and has given it the name 'Shivering Mountain'. Carry on for ³⁄₄ mile, passing a track joining from the left and shortly thereafter going through a gate **E**.

Immediately turn through a second gate on the right and choose the most right of the two signed paths, which hugs the western wall. At the distant narrowing of the field, ignore a wooden gate and continue through the metal gate ahead. Climb at the edge of the next field past a diminutive dew pond to find a small waymarked gate tucked by a kink in the boundary **F**. Through

| 0 | 200 | 400 | 600 | 800 METRES | 1 |
| 0 | 200 | 400 | 600 YARDS | ½ | KILOMETRES MILES |

that, the path sticks with a wall across the shoulder of the hill below Starvehouse Mine. Many of the names attached to the old lead workings hint of disappointment and hardship and, even if a rich strike brought huge profits for the owners, the comparative pittance for the labouring miners was always hard-earned with danger never far away.

Beyond a gate, the way becomes enclosed, but there are expansive views to the west and, even from this distance, Eldon Hole remains readily distinguishable. Approaching a farm, bypass it to the left, leaving the hillside through a gate to join its service track. Developing as a quiet lane, it offers pleasant walking in a rolling landscape of chequered pasture all the way back to Old Dam, one mile away. Turn left back to Peak Forest. ●

Stanage Edge

		GPS waypoints
Start	Upper Burbage Bridge	SK 260 830
Distance	5½ miles (8.9km)	Ⓐ SK 250 830
Height gain	900 feet (274m)	Ⓑ SK 244 835
Approximate time	2½ hours	Ⓒ SK 238 845
Parking	Car park west of bridge	Ⓓ SK 227 843
Route terrain	Clear moorland paths, rugged track and lane	Ⓔ SK 244 829
Ordnance Survey maps	Landranger 110 (Sheffield & Huddersfield), Explorer OL1 (The Peak District – Dark Peak area)	

Meaning simply 'Stone Edge', Stanage is part of the long gritstone escarpment bounding the eastern rim of the Derwent Valley. Easily attained, this superb, high-level stroll is full of dramatic interest every step of the way, descending an ancient highway to return along quiet country lanes.

Leaving the car park, follow the roadside verge left to a sharp bend, where a path strikes ahead across the moor towards the southern abutment of Stanage Edge, some ¼ mile away. Approaching the rocky defences, the Cowper Stone becomes prominent to the right, a huge, detached boulder of

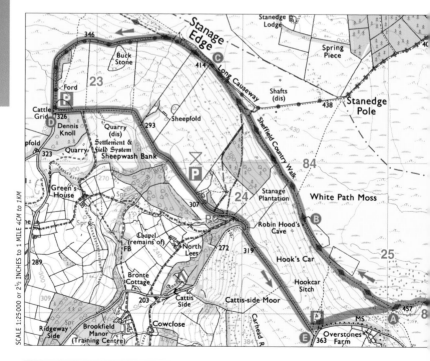

gritstone, which offers a challenge to the most experienced rock climbers. Just about every nook and cranny along Stanage's 4-mile (6.4km) length offers a route to the top, encompassing all levels of difficulty from a simple scramble to extremely severe. Although barely 100 feet high, it embodies Britain's longest climbing route, a complete end-to-end traverse. There is nothing so demanding on this walk and the route soon clambers onto the escarpment, where a slabbed path forking left leads towards the trig point Ⓐ.

Before the last war, the cliffs lay within the Duke of Rutland's grouse shoot and both climbers and ramblers had to keep a wary eye open to avoid the sometimes aggressive discouragements of his gamekeepers. In earlier times, the rock was valued for more practical purposes, its hard, gritty surface rendering it ideal for use as millstones. Great circular 'cheeses' of stone were quarried from the cliffs, but not all were carted away and many still lie among the heather of the lower slopes.

Picking its way among the boulders littering the ridge, the route meanders above the crevices and notches fracturing the cliff below. The superb panorama extends across the Derwent and Hope Valleys, bounded on the western horizon by the plateau of Kinder Scout, the loftiest height of the Peak District National Park. Closer to is Mam Tor and Lose Hill, with the

The Cowper Stone

distinctive peaky top of Win Hill to the right. To the north, the spike of Stanedge Pole breaks the emptiness of the moor, an ancient marker along a highway climbing from Sheffield into Derwent. Records note its existence from the middle of the 16th century, although the tall wooden post is obviously not the original.

After walking ½ mile, watch out for a path branching off left Ⓑ, which drops along an easy rocky gully to a ledge part way down, where you will find a hollow known as Robin Hood's Cave. You can crawl through to a rocky platform, which has a stunning outlook across the landscape.

Climb back to the main path and continue along the ridge, eventually merging with a rough track Ⓒ. It is the old highway previously mentioned, which you can follow to see Stanedge Pole at first hand. Ahead, the track makes a leisurely descent from the ridge, curving to meet a metalled lane at the corner of Dennis Knoll Ⓓ.

The way back to Upper Burbage Bridge lies to the left, keeping left again at successive junctions. Reaching a vergeside parking area beside the second road junction Ⓔ, you have a choice of routes for the final leg. *As an alternative to the last mile left along the road, you can follow an easy path to regain the ridge near the trig point and return along your outward route.* ●

Rowarth to Cown Edge

Start	Rowarth near New Mills	**GPS waypoints**	
Distance	5¾ miles (9.3km)		SK 011 892
Height gain	840 feet (256m)	**A**	SK 012 893
Approximate time	2½ hours	**B**	SK 008 909
Parking	Car park in village	**C**	SK 014 910
Route terrain	Field trods and lanes	**D**	SK 021 922
Ordnance Survey maps	Landranger 110 (Sheffield & Huddersfield), Explorer OL1 (The Peak District – Dark Peak area)	**E**	SK 022 904
		F	SK 023 895

Tucked in a quiet valley above New Mills, Rowarth is typical of the attractive farming hamlets dotting the peripheral western Peakland slopes. The walk climbs over Cown Edge, a high rocky vantage above the rural suburbs of Stockport, taking in an ancient curiosity romantically called 'Robin Hood's Picking Rods'.

Rowarth's handful of sturdy stone cottages stand below a long snout, that rises to a prominent ridge overlooking the western plain. Farming, stone quarrying and hand-loom weaving all contributed to the valley economy, and a 17th-century mill was converted for the manufacture of candlewicks. Although washed away by a great flood

Robin Hood's Picking Rods

in 1930, part of the building still stands as the **Little Mill Inn**, where a restored waterwheel is a picturesque attraction.

Leaving the car park, turn right into the village. Keep ahead past a junction, but just beyond the cottages, look for a narrow, fenced passage on the left **A**. A clear trod continues steadily upwards, shortly intercepting a track beside a five-way fingerpost. Bearing left, cross the track and continue up the gorse-flecked hillside, pocked with the scars of old mineral workings. Over a stile, keep by the left boundary above Near Slack Farm and carry on to its neighbour, Far Slack Farm. Walk past the farm to meet a crossing track **B**. Robin Hood's Picking Rods then lie some 300 yds to the left, two sturdy truncated stone pillars set in a mighty boulder.

Robin of Loxley's exploits range far beyond the traditional Sherwood Forest. The story here tells of a remarkable feat of bowmanship to rescue a fair damsel from a heartless uncle in Longdendale

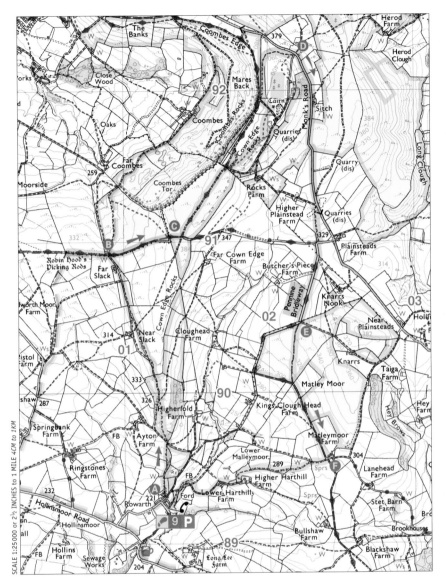

SCALE 1:25000 or 2½ INCHES to 1 MILE 4CM to 1KM

who had forbidden her marriage to the love of her life. Despite Robin siding to her cause, the uncle remained obstinate and, thinking to settle the matter, devised a seemingly impossible archery contest, the target being the distant cross on Cown Edge. The outlaws took up the challenge and all arrows found the mark, Robin's own flèche striking

with such tremendous force that its gouge remains visible today. The stones may have been old even in Robin's time and it is probable that they are the stumps of Saxon crosses, perhaps marking a boundary or a path across the hills.

Retrace your steps to the junction by Far Slack Farm **B** and keep ahead along a rising path. Doglegging through a gate, continue to the crest of the hill. Cross a stile on the left **C**, and head out

Knarrs Nook

on a trod towards a woodland plantation. Over another stile there, bear right above the grassy rim of Cown Edge Rocks from which there is an unrivalled view across to Kinder and, farther north, the moorland mass of Bleaklow. After skirting above a small quarry, drop to a sunken path and follow it left to a junction of walls and paths.

Turn right though a gap and walk away with a broken wall on your left and more trees over to your right. Passing beyond the corner of the plantation, veer from the wall to lose height through a fold. Curve right across the grassy slope, dropping to leave over a couple of stiles onto Monk's Road **D**.

Follow the lane right for a little over ¹⁄₂ mile to a reach track leading off to Higher Plainstead and Rocks farms. Scale a wall stile beside the entrance and strike a shallow diagonal to another stile in the bottom far-right corner of the field. Emerging at a junction, take the metalled lane opposite, signed as the Pennine Bridleway to Lantern Pike and Hayfield. Where it later bends sharply right **E**, cross the stile ahead and trace an onward path across the heather. Through a small gate at the far side of the heath, bear left along a gated track, which leads to a junction beside Matleymoor Farm **F**.

Take a short grass track right and carry on by the right-hand wall of a field. Over a stile in the corner maintain your direction across the hillside, soon joining a wall on the left. Keep going over more stiles, beyond which a green track develops. Reaching the field corner, swing left, dropping to a gate and stile beside a barn at Higher Farm.

Signed right to Rowarth, a concrete track descends the hillside into a wooded valley. Lower down, a ford can be avoided by diverting over a footbridge on the right. Rejoining the concrete track just below the ford, cross to a stile opposite from which a path runs on above the stream. Carry on through a narrow gate to emerge in Rowarth beside a red telephone box. Go right to a junction and then turn left back to the car park. ●

Lord's Seat

		GPS waypoints
Start	Barber Booth	🖉 SK 107 847
Distance	5½ miles (8.9km)	Ⓐ SK 111 846
Height gain	1,150 feet (351m)	Ⓑ SK 106 840
Approximate time	3 hours	Ⓒ SK 099 829
Parking	Car park west of hamlet beyond railway viaduct	Ⓓ SK 112 834
		Ⓔ SK 124 834
Route terrain	Moorland paths and tracks, *take care in mist*	Ⓕ SK 124 846
Ordnance Survey maps	Landranger 110 (Sheffield & Huddersfield), Explorer OL1 (The Peak District – Dark Peak area)	

Edale is ringed by high hills, all blessed with superb views. But one of the best vantages is Lord's Seat, which can be attained with only a modest effort. Joining the old road out of the valley to Chapel-en-le-Frith, the route climbs to a shallow saddle and then follows a broad shoulder rising onto the top. Beyond the summit, the path falls along a narrowing grass ridge to Mam Nick then drops from the hill to saunter back across the fields. Alternatively, you can combine this route with that of Walk 20 to continue along the ridge all the way to Lose Hill.

🖉 From the Barber Booth car park, walk back along the lane beneath the railway viaduct. After another 100 yds look for a stile beside a gate on the right Ⓐ. A path heads beside a stream towards Manor House Farm, later slipping across the brook before turning out to a track. Mount a stile opposite, head to the far corner of a paddock and skirt derelict outbuildings to reach the field beyond. Carry on by the boundary to a gate and then strike a diagonal course across more fields to a gate at the top of the intake Ⓑ.

Emerging onto a rough track, turn right through a second gate and fork left to follow Chapel Gate, which rises steadily across the northern flank of the hill. After ½ mile, as you pass a path signed off to Upper Booth and Hayfield,

the gradient levels, the track continuing for a further ¼ mile to a junction of paths in front of a wall Ⓒ. The path left is signed to Castleton and Hope via Mam Tor, and follows the wall for ¾ mile to the top of Lord's Seat Ⓓ.

A raised grass platform to the left of the path is a Bronze Age tumulus, and affords a superb view in every direction. Bounding the opposite side of the Vale of Edale is the steep southern flank of the Kinder plateau, deeply incised by dramatic cloughs that gnaw far back into the hill. To the south lie the limestone hills and dales of the White Peak, prominent among which are the gaunt cliffs of Eldon Hill, which were created by quarrying to produce gravel for road construction.

Although apparently out of the way,

Edale offered a passage between east and west, with packhorse tracks climbing out at the head of the valley to both Chapel-en-le-Frith and Hayfield. It also provided a convenient corridor for a trans-Pennine railway link between Sheffield and Manchester. Work began on the 21-mile line between Dore and Chinley in 1888 and was completed in 1894. The route required two tunnels;

Looking east from Cown Edge

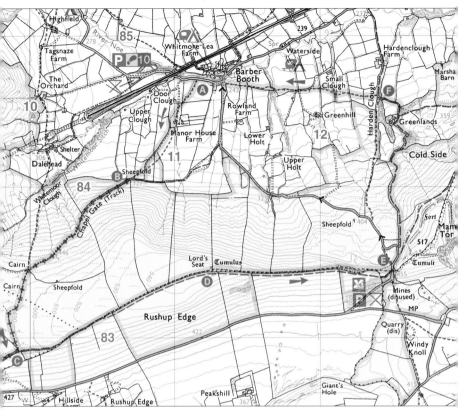

SCALE 1:25000 or 2½ INCHES to 1 MILE 4CM to 1KM

| 0 | 200 | 400 | 600 | 800 METRES | 1 |
| 0 | 200 | 400 | 600 YARDS | ½ | KILOMETRES MILES |

Totley, which took the line from Sheffield into the Derwent Valley and another here to break out of the head of Edale. The Cowburn Tunnel, which begins in the cutting below Barber Booth at your feet, is 3,702 yds long and emerges on the western side of the hill above Chapel Milton. The line operated in competition to the Woodhead railway farther north, which had been opened 50 years earlier. Despite a considerable post-war investment in electrification and new tunnels, Woodhead was eventually closed in 1981. However, this remains a busy commuter line and offers walkers a chance to leave the car at home.

The path runs on beyond the summit, gradually falling more steeply. The ridge progressively narrows before falling abruptly to the lane at Mam Nick **E**. You could, of course, simply return along the lane, but a more pleasant route follows a bridlepath, beginning at a gate by the bus stop, a short way down to the left.

Through the gate branch left and head straight down the hill. Eventually, after curving before a communications mast, the path drops past a large house, Greenlands. Just beyond the house, abandon the path through a gate on the left and follow the drive downhill. Winding through a wooded clough, cross a stream and then immediately climb to a stile on the left **F**. Head straight out from field to field, later crossing another deep clough and ultimately emerging at a junction below Barber Booth. The lane opposite, signed to Upper Booth soon returns you to the car park. ●

Chinley Head

		GPS waypoints
Start	Chinley	🥾 SK 040 827
Distance	5½ miles (8.9km)	Ⓐ SK 035 827
Height gain	1,250 feet (381m)	Ⓑ SK 039 830
Approximate time	3 hours	Ⓒ SK 038 834
Parking	Roadside parking in village	Ⓓ SK 036 842
Route terrain	Hill paths and tracks	Ⓔ SK 048 851
Ordnance Survey maps	Landranger 110 (Sheffield & Huddersfield), Explorer OL1 (The Peak District – Dark Peak area)	Ⓕ SK 056 846
		Ⓖ SK 051 834

Chinley lies at the foot of a grassy side-valley on the edge of the Peak District's western hills, its slopes rising either side to give grand views across the surrounding countryside. The walk ascends Chinley Churn, whose upper terrace was once extensively quarried for stone, and continues around the head of the vale of Otterbrook to return along an old track across its eastern flank.

Before the construction of the Peak Forest Canal to Whaley Bridge, Chinley, then known as Maynestonefield was little more than a hamlet. A horse-drawn tramway was built along the Blackbrook Valley connecting the waterway with limestone quarries at Dove Holes, beyond Chapel-en-le-Frith. It also opened a market for the high quality, close-grained gritstone outcropping above Chinley on Cracken Edge, which was sought after for roofing and paving tiles. The dawning industrial age saw the construction of three mills taking their power from the swift-flowing Black Brook, but it was the arrival of the railway in 1867 that really prompted expansion and gave the place its present name, Chinley. Lines to Manchester, London and Sheffield all met here and it became an important junction. The town's proximity to Manchester also made it an attractive proposition to moneyed Victorian commuters, who built their comfortable villas in a country setting away from the grime and overcrowding of the city.

🥾 The walk begins from the centre of the village, just east of the station at the junction of Green Lane with the

The quarries of Cracken Edge

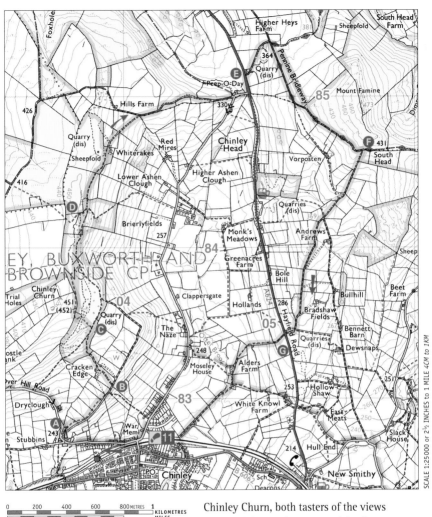

SCALE 1:25000 or 2½ INCHES to 1 MILE 4CM to 1KM

0	200	400	600	800 METRES	1

KILOMETRES
MILES

0	200	400	600 YARDS	½

main street, the B6062. Follow Green Lane over a railway bridge to the war memorial and turn left along Stubbins Lane. Beyond houses, the lane gains height past Chinley Park and then bends in front of a junction. A short distance after that, look for a waymarked track leaving on the right **A**.

It climbs steeply past a communications mast as a sunken way, but higher up there are glimpses across the Blackbrook Valley to Eccles Pike and on the left to Cracken Edge, the quarried cliffs fringing the summit of Chinley Churn, both tasters of the views to be had during the course of the day. After a good ¼ mile, leave along a waymarked, gated track on the left **B**.

As the track bends to a farm, walk ahead on a rising grass trod beside a second farm to a small gate. Keep with the left wall to another gate and climb the gorse-covered hillside. Intercepting a broader path, follow it right, soon approaching a fence and stile. However, some 20 yds before there **C**, swing off left on a trod that inclines to the foot of the quarries. Now turn right to meet the same fence you encountered lower down. Immediately over the stile, a faint path beside the fence finds an easy

Whiterakes

passage onto the top of the cliffs.

Head north in a delightful saunter along the edge of the cliffs, soaking up the panorama across the Chinley Valley. Beyond the head is Kinder Scout, while behind to the south west is Shining Tor, which overlooks the upper reaches of the Goyt Valley. Reaching a wall, cross the stile, but at the next wall **D**, ignore the inviting gap. Instead, drop beside the wall, zigzagging down beyond its corner to reach a broad path below the scarp.

Follow it left, descending easily towards Whiterakes. Keep with the main track beyond the abandoned farmstead as it arcs right, losing height through a couple of fields to meet another track. To the right, it leads out to the main road beside Peep-O-Day Farm, so named because it catches the first glimmer of the dawn sun rising as it breaks free of the eastern hills.

Follow the verges 150 yds to the left, crossing to a bridleway beside a cottage, Chinley Moor House **E**. After curving past a small quarry, walk up to meet another track. Signed right as the Pennine Bridleway to South Head, it rises easily across the flank of the forlornly named Mount Famine. Stay with it, later bending left past a couple of gates and passing through the gates of a sheep pen a few yards farther on. Keep going beside a wall until, at an intermediate crest, you reach a gate into the National Trust land of South Head **F**.

Do not go through, but instead mount a step stile just before it. Accompany the wall straight down the hill, crossing another stile lower down. Passing through a gap at the bottom of the field, the track swings left, but you should keep ahead along a narrowing intake to another field. Stick by the left wall above Andrews Farm, shortly joining its access track, which eventually leads out to the main road **G**.

Cross to a stile opposite from which a sunken path continues down the hillside. Through a gate at the bottom, bear left towards Alders Farm. Leave the field through a second gate and walk past the house to join a rough track leading away. After passing beneath the railway, it ultimately emerges onto the B6062 on the edge of Chinley. Go right back to the village centre. ●

Redmires Reservoirs

		GPS waypoints
Start	Wyming Brook	🖉 SK 268 858
Distance	6 miles (9.7km)	Ⓐ SK 271 855
Height gain	850 feet (259m)	Ⓑ SK 274 853
Approximate time	3 hours	Ⓒ SK 276 845
Parking	Car park at start	Ⓓ SK 256 851
Route terrain	Generally clear paths across open moorland and woodland	Ⓔ SK 256 856
		Ⓕ SK 257 873
		Ⓖ SK 264 870
Ordnance Survey maps	Landranger 110 (Sheffield & Huddersfield), Explorer OL1 (The Peak District – Dark Peak area)	

Hallam Moors lie barely a mile (1.6km) from the suburbs of Sheffield, yet the heather slopes and forested valleys are a world apart from the populous city. The walk begins along the deserted flanks of Rud Hill above the Redmires Reservoirs and then loops back through the mixed woodlands above the neighbouring Rivelin Valley.

The outbreak of the First World War in 1914 saw many local battalions formed across the country, patriotic fervour and a belief that the war would be over in months bringing no shortage of willing volunteers. Recruiting began on 10 September for the 12th (Service) Battalion of the York and Lancaster

Regiment, better known as the Sheffield Pals. Within two days, more than 1,000 local men from all walks of life had joined up. Initial instruction began in the town, but the approach of winter saw the regiment encamped in wooden huts above Redmires with Lancashire lads from Burnley and Accrington. Conditions were harsh as the men were trained in drill, trench digging and the

Redmires Lower Reservoir

Reddicar Clough

rudiments of combat, but this helped form a strong bond between them. In May, the Pals were moved to scarcely better conditions on Cannock Chase for further military instruction and, after several more postings, were shipped off to Egypt at the end of the year to defend the Suez Canal against a Turkish threat.

The attack never materialised and in the spring of 1916, the battalion was posted to the front line in France. Troops were being massed for a mammoth push against the German lines of the Somme, the Sheffield lads being given the task of taking the small but strategic village of Serre. The massive attack began early on 1 July but within minutes the futility of it all must have been obvious as thousands of men were mown down by machine gun fire. By the end of the first horrific day, almost 600 of the Sheffield Pals had been killed or wounded. The carnage dragged on until November, during which time more than $1\frac{1}{2}$ million men, British, Empire, French and German lost their lives. Although subsequently reinforced, the Pals never recovered and were finally disbanded early in 1918. A memorial stands in the French village of Serre to the Sheffield men who never came home.

✎ Leaving the car park, cross Wyming Brook and head up the hill. At the top, turn into Soughley Lane

walking as far as a sharp left bend to find a stile on the right Ⓐ. Follow a track towards the foot of Lower Redmires going left at the end of the wall, over a stile and uphill once more. As the track levels, keep on until halted by a gate Ⓑ. Mount the stile on the right and walk away at the field edge. Meeting a farm track from Fulwood Booth, turn left past the mounds of an old quarry and follow it out to a lane. Go right, later rounding a bend to leave over a ladder-stile on the right Ⓒ.

Contrary to the line shown on some Ordnance Survey maps, the permitted path takes the right-most of two gates at the far end of the grass track to climb past a storage cistern in the adjacent field. A ladder-stile in the corner advances the path onto the moor, striking to a second stile in a fence ahead. Although initially faint, the way soon gathers tangibility to undulate westward past occasional marker posts across the heather and peat of Rud Hill. Almost straight ahead on the skyline rises the slender staff of Stanedge Pole, while below are the three Redmires Reservoirs, backed by forest plantation.

The peat later gives way to bouldery heath and, above the upper reservoir, the path curves in gentle descent towards its head, shortly passing a boundary stone. Cut with the initials SWW, it was erected by Sheffield Water Works when they constructed the reservoirs in the middle of the 19th century. The path drops to a stile beside a footbridge spanning Fairthorn Clough, across which it leads out to a byway Ⓓ.

Follow it above the head of the upper reservoir to a small car park, immediately beyond which a path is signed off through a hand-gate Ⓔ. It rises beside plantation to rough grazing above, following a wall past an old quarry, which provided stone for the reservoir, and then fording a stream.

Over a second rise, continue beyond the wall corner, shortly accompanying another wall to a bridged ditch. Cross the stile next to the gate in front and carry on along a clear path. After the wall curves away, walk on past an isolated clump of rhododendron to reach a waymarked crossing of paths **F**.

Go right along the crest of Head Stone Bank from which there is a glimpse of the Rivelin Reservoir through a gap in the trees. At a fork bear right, dropping towards woodland in Reddicar Clough. The path winds into the thick of the trees, eventually meeting a broad path, Wyming Brook Drive. Follow it right to a bridge spanning Reddicar Brook, immediately after which, a rough path leaves on the right **G**.

Climbing stiffly, it soon crosses the accompanying stream and then swings sharply left on an easier line to the top of the trees. Breaking cover, the way undulates along the steep bank above the forest margin, later dipping into the fringe of trees before finally curving away across the moor to meet the corner of a wall. Pass around the corner and walk on with the wall on your right, eventually losing height to return to the car park. ●

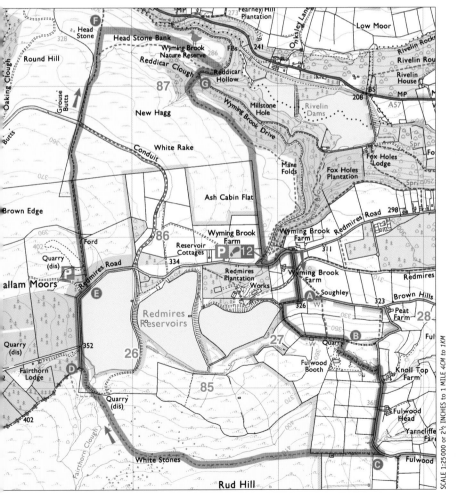

Lyme Park

Start	Lyme Park		GPS waypoints
Distance	6 miles (9.7km)		🏁 SJ 963 823
Height gain	1,000 feet (305m)		Ⓐ SJ 966 830
			Ⓑ SJ 972 821
Approximate time	3 hours		Ⓒ SJ 973 812
Parking	Car park at start		Ⓓ SJ 971 807
Route terrain	Open parkland, moorland paths and tracks		Ⓔ SJ 954 805
			Ⓕ SJ 948 814
Dog friendly	Dogs should be kept on leads within deer park		Ⓖ SJ 949 816
Ordnance Survey maps	Landranger 110 (Sheffield & Huddersfield), Explorer OL1 (The Peak District – Dark Peak area)		

Lyme Park lies at the edge of the Peak District overlooking the northern Cheshire plain and, although now almost touched by the fringes of the Greater Manchester conurbation, it encompasses a surprisingly vast area of rough grassy hills. This energetic walk traces the high moorland boundary of the estate and is rewarded by extensive panoramas across markedly contrasting landscapes.

For nearly 600 years Lyme Hall belonged to the Legh family, but in 1946 Richard Legh, gave the hall and

park to the National Trust. The present mansion replaces an earlier medieval hall and was built during the Tudor period, but then remodelled in the Palladian style in the 1720s by the

Cluse Hay

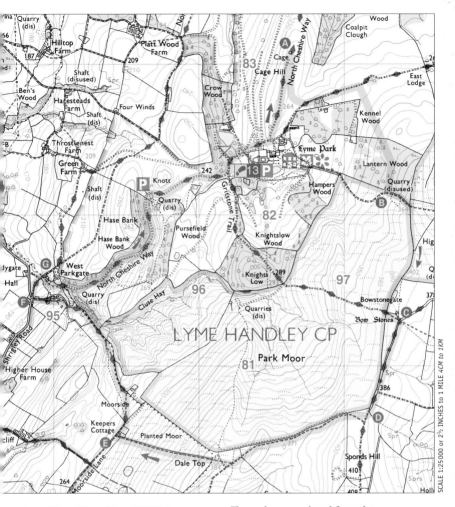

The park was enclosed from the surrounding Macclesfield Forest in 1346 as a private deer park and soon became noted for its fine herd of red deer. Hunting was a popular sport for the Leghs and the Cage was built in the 16th century as a lookout for the ladies to watch the proceedings in comfort. Deer still roam freely across the 1,300 acres (525 ha) of the estate, although they are not always easy to see.

Italian architect Giacomo Leoni. Its character reflects 18th-century taste and is a treasure trove of fine paintings, furnishings and tapestries.

🖉 Leave the car park by the information centre, taking a stepped path to the garden and house. Reaching the courtyard gates, turn away left, and walk across a junction. Abandon the drive almost immediately, on the bend, and climb a trod ahead. It rises between a sparse avenue of trees along the broad back of a long, grassy hill to a square tower at its far end known as the Cage Ⓐ.

At the foot of the Cage, double back sharp right on a lower trod, falling along the flank of the hill below the outward path. Before long, a swathe provides a path left across the heath to meet the drive, which you should then follow left

The Cage

past Kennel Wood. Approaching a circular clump of trees, bear off to a fence stile on the right and climb the hill to find a ladder-stile mounting the high wall surrounding Lantern Wood. Walk through the trees, passing above the Lantern, a folly built of stones taken from the Elizabethan hall. Leave the wood at its far end over another ladder-stile, back onto the bare hillside Ⓑ.

Follow the wall up the hill to the top of the wood, turning within the shallow corner to continue along the eastern boundary of the estate. The view extends across the Cheshire plain, where landmarks such as the Jodrell Bank telescope and Alderley Edge can be seen, with the distant hills behind them belonging to Wales. Farther around to the right is the Wirral peninsula and Merseyside, while the conurbation of Greater Manchester nestles at the foot of the Pennine hills.

Marking the high point of the estate, a topograph identifies some of the surrounding features, its plinth extending the panorama by allowing you to see to the east over the tall wall. Keep going until you reach a ladder-stile by a gate, passing out of the park

beside a lonely farmhouse to emerge onto the end of a lane Ⓒ.

Just to the left beside the lane are the Bow Stones, believed to be part of the shafts of late Saxon crosses and might have been set here to serve as landmarks or boundary stones. The onward route, however, lies to the right, following a gated, walled track along the hilltop for some 700 yds before breaking out onto the open moor Ⓓ.

Leave the track there, sticking by the right-hand wall; the way signed to Pott Shrigley. Losing height, a track eventually develops which later parts company with the wall and leads to a gate. Just beyond, bear off right, climbing the grassy spoil heaps of old workings to a waymarked fence stile at Dale Top. Over that, walk straight ahead down the hill, guided by a stone wall on your right. Keep going to the bottom to gain a track, Moorside Lane at Keepers Cottage Ⓔ.

Walk right past the cottage and then look for a wall stile by a gate on the left. Signed to Higher Poynton, a trod strikes a shallow diagonal over open grass, later dipping across a tree-lined gully. The continuing path curves to join a wall above a deepening clough, eventually dropping beside an old quarry before emerging onto the end of a track by some houses. Follow it out to a lane beside Green Close Methodist Church Ⓕ.

Go right and then immediately leave the lane along another track, crossing a bridge to West Parkgate Lodge Ⓖ. Turn in front of it through a gate back into the National Trust estate and follow a delightful track winding up a wooded valley, which higher up, in early summer, is ablaze with the colourful flowers of rhododendron. Beyond another gate at the top, carry on with the drive through open parkland to return to the car park below the house. ●

Broomhead Reservoir

		GPS waypoints
Start	Bolsterstone	🖉 SK 270 967
Distance	6 miles (9.7km)	Ⓐ SK 269 963
Height gain	1,000 feet (305m)	Ⓑ SK 272 958
Approximate time	3 hours	Ⓒ SK 255 959
Parking	By village church	Ⓓ SK 248 957
Route terrain	Woodland and field paths and good tracks	Ⓔ SK 241 962
		Ⓕ SK 241 969
Ordnance Survey maps	Landranger 110 (Sheffield & Huddersfield), Explorer OL1 (The Peak District – Dark Peak area)	

The adjacent valleys of the Little Don and Ewden could hardly be more different, the one home to what was once one of the largest steel works in England while in the other, forest drapes the valley side above a couple of lakes. From the tiny village of Bolsterstone, the route is one of downs and ups, first dropping beside the Broomhead Reservoir, climbing to the parkland of Broomhead Hall and then descending to cross the valley at Ewden Bridge. A final climb through woodland and grazing returns the walk along the broad ridge dividing the two valleys, an enjoyable stroll heightened by extensive views.

The tiny village of Bolsterstone traces its origins to Saxon times and stood on an ancient packhorse trail along which salt was brought from Cheshire. The

Beside the Broomhead Reservoir

St Mary's Church and the Bolsterstones

substantial bolster stones themselves are to be found in the churchyard, removed there for safekeeping from the village green in the 19th century. Their origin is obscure, although it has been suggested they might have been the base of either a gibbet or a double cross. Other relics in the village include the stocks by the lychgate and an old water pump and trough beside the village hall, which was formerly the National School and built in 1852.

Head south out of the village past the village hall. At a junction, bear right and go steeply downhill, keeping right again at a second fork lower down. After 200 yds, look for a path signed off on the left Ⓐ, which drops through a wood. Crossing a stream, turn left and follow its bank to a small service reservoir, from where a broader path falls to meet a track by a wood-boarded cottage. Follow that left past houses to reach a lane. Carry on downhill to a junction, taking the lane opposite and crossing the outflow from the Broomhead Reservoir.

Leave on the bend beyond, where a footpath is signed into Horse Wood Ⓑ. It rises gently through the trees, passing

the dam to continue above the Broomhead Reservoir. Eventually the path meets a lane, but you can avoid the tarmac by hugging the wooded shore. After ¹⁄₂ mile, a wooden walkway takes the path across a stream, Lee Lane Dike. At the end of the planking, leave through a gap in the fence Ⓒ and cross to a broad track opposite. Climb through the forest to emerge on Allas Lane and carry on up the hill. After passing a gateway into Broomhead Park, and before reaching a road junction, leave over a waymarked wall stile on the right Ⓓ.

Bear right from the wall across a couple of streams, beyond which a waymark directs you towards a gate where fence and wall meet. Continuing through more gates, follow a fence up the slope towards Broomhead Hall, which soon comes into view. The way remains in the field, bypassing farm cottages to a wall stile in the corner. A path ushers you to a track, which in turn, leads out to a lane Ⓔ.

Head steeply downhill to cross Ewden

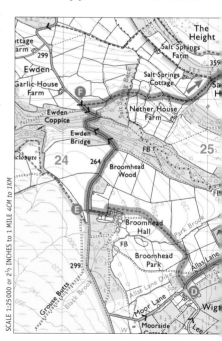

SCALE 1:25000 or 2½ INCHES to 1 MILE 4CM to 1KM

Bridge and climb the equally severe gradient beyond. After walking 150 yds beyond a sharp left-hand bend, look for a footpath signed off through a field-gate on the right 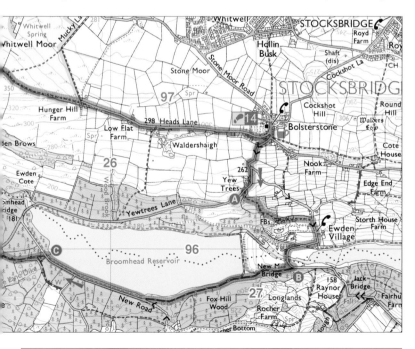. Bear right across the field, taking the prominent rounded hill on the skyline above as your mark. Through a gate keep going between the trees and across a stream. Stay above a bracken bank, picking up an obvious path through a belt of wood. Ignore a crossing path higher up and continue over a stile. The way angles ever-upwards through bracken and gorse scrub, making for the top corner of another plantation.

There, the path turns up beside a wall, passing through a gateway to join a rough track from Salt Springs Cottage and Farm. Follow it over the crest of the hill, where it then turns alongside the edge of Whitwell Moor. Gently descending for $1\frac{1}{2}$ miles along the spine of a broad ridge, from which there are views over the valley and across to neighbouring Stocksbridge, it eventually leads back to Bolsterstone.

The town of Stocksbridge lies just to the north, overlooking the massive steel works that run along the base of the valley for much of its length. Before Samuel Fox arrived in 1842 looking for a suitable place to set up a wire drawing mill, the settlement had a population of only 34. Fox began his business in an abandoned corn mill, producing wire for the manufacture of pins and later for his 'Paragon' folding umbrella frame, which he invented in 1851. His firm went on to develop a range of specialised products, which included railway lines, springs for Rolls Royce and, later, steels for the aviation industry. Such was the scale of business, that in 1872 a branch line was brought into the valley to service the mills, which, at their peak, employed over 7,000 people. The works are now owned by Corus, part of the Indian steel giant, Tata, and, despite a downturn in the industry and clouds of threatened closure, plans have now been put forward for investment to produce hi-tech steels for the aerospace industry. ●

Shatton Moor

		GPS waypoints	
Start	Shatton	📷	SK 203 825
Distance	6 miles (9.7km)	Ⓐ	SK 197 823
Height gain	1,200 feet (366m)	Ⓑ	SK 187 823
Approximate time	3 hours	Ⓒ	SK 181 826
Parking	Roadside parking on Shatton Lane near bridge over River Noe	Ⓓ	SK 183 820
		Ⓔ	SK 183 802
Route terrain	Lane and upland tracks	Ⓕ	SK 199 823
Ordnance Survey maps	Landranger 110 (Sheffield & Huddersfield), Explorer OL1 (The Peak District – Dark Peak area)		

The high ground of Shatton Moor lies on the shale buffer between the dark gritstone of the north and east and the limestone that forms the southern heart of the Peak. Although demanding an energetic pull onto the tops, this circuit from the hamlet around the head of Over Dale is otherwise without difficulty and follows quiet lanes and clear tracks throughout.

📷 Park beside the lane near the bridge at the bottom of Shatton and walk up into the village. Swing right at the first junction and continue to the top of the street, where you will find a stile into the field beyond. Bear left to another stile in the far corner and carry on at the edge of the subsequent fields before descending a stepped bank onto the narrow sunken way of Townfield Lane Ⓐ. Follow it to the right for nearly ¹/₂ mile, until it turns down to Shatton Hall Farm.

Leaving it there, slip through the gate on the right and walk on along a gravel track beside the hedge. Towards the far end of the field, that track in turn swings left to Elmore Hill Farm through a gate Ⓑ.

At this point, there is a choice of routes, dependent upon whether you wish to visit the site of a Roman fort in the valley. For the fort, keep ahead to another gate in the corner of the field, from which a track descends steeply

through a strip of pine plantation. At a fork lower down, keep ahead on the metalled Brough Lane, dropping out to the B6049 road at the edge of Brough. Immediately over the bridge to the left, a path off on the right rises across a field to the square, grass platform, the site of Navio, the Roman fort Ⓒ.

Overlooking the confluence of Bradwell Brook with the River Noe stood Navio. Sadly, not too much is known of its history and there is little left to see, but it is a place for imaginative souls to envisage the scene in this then remote valley, almost two millennia ago. Encompassing more than 2 acres (0.8 hectares), it was founded around AD70 and originally defended by a simple wooden stockade. Evidence suggests it might then have been abandoned before subsequently being rebuilt in stone around the middle of the 2nd century. It was connected to Buxton by the Roman road of Batham Gate through the Bradwell Valley, while another road ran

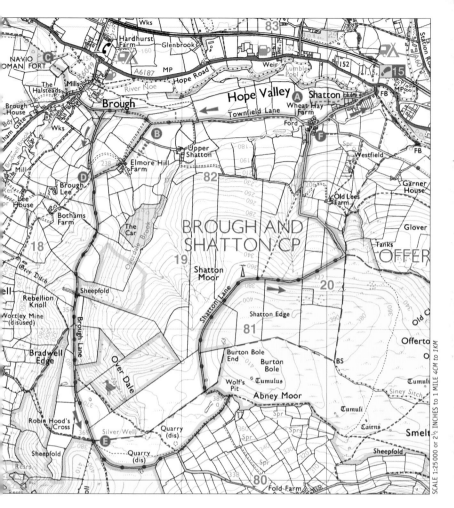

north-west to a fort at Melandra, on the edge of the Pennine hills near present-day Glossop. Apart from maintaining order among the native British tribes in the area, the fort had some strategic importance in overseeing the mining and smelting of lead, of which there were extensive outcrops hereabouts. It appears that the military fort was finally abandoned around AD360, but, as with most Roman camps, a civilian settlement grew up around its walls. A thermal spring and Roman bath house was discovered just along the road at Bradwell when foundations were being dug at the beginning of the 19th century for an inn. This still stands and is appropriately named the New Bath Hotel.

To continue the route, retrace your steps up Brough Lane to the fork and now go right, climbing steeply for ¼ mile to meet the alternative path coming in above Elmore Hill Farm **D**.

If you are not visiting the fort, you can instead follow the track from **B**, *left to Elmore Hill Farm.* Cross the yard to another gate in the top right corner and go left, over the access drive to head away at the field edge over the shoulder of the hill, the way signed to Bradwell. Leave the corner of the field over a stile to join Brough Lane **D**.

Continue steeply up the hill for $\frac{1}{2}$ mile before the gradient starts to ease, pausing to enjoy the views over the valley of the Bradwell Brook on the one hand and the deep moorland cleft of Over Dale on the other. Eventually the track arrives at a gate at Robin Hood's Cross **E**.

Beyond the way curves around the head of Over Dale briefly following the watershed. Carry on past the track off right into Abney Clough, staying with the main track as it eventually settles a course below Shatton Edge towards a radio mast. Now roughly metalled, the way begins to fall ever more steeply, after a while dropping into the woodland of the lower slopes. The lane ultimately leads to a junction at Wheat Hay Farm **F**. *You can then simply turn right and follow the lane through the village back to the bridge or go left, crossing a ford to find the field path by which you began the walk, just a little way along on the right* **A**. ●

Across the Hope Valley to Bamford Moor

Digley Reservoir

		GPS waypoints	
Start	Digley Reservoir	🖉	SE 109 067
Distance	6¼ miles (10.1km)	Ⓐ	SE 110 071
Height gain	1,075 feet (328m)	Ⓑ	SE 093 073
Approximate time	3 hours	Ⓒ	SE 086 072
Parking	Car park at start	Ⓓ	SE 087 060
Route terrain	Mainly upland tracks, occasionally rough, *take care in mist*	Ⓔ	SE 107 060
Ordnance Survey maps	Landranger 110 (Sheffield & Huddersfield), Explorer OL1 (The Peak District – Dark Peak area)		

Beginning from the Digley Reservoir car park, this fine walk encircles its main tributaries of Marsden Clough and Hey Clough below the steeply rising slopes of Black Hill. It makes use of old trackways, which connected the many isolated farms that once dotted the hillside and whose ruins now stand as reminders of a way of life long gone.

🖉 Out of the car park, follow the lane over the dam. At a junction beyond go left, but as the road then bends, leave through a kissing-gate Ⓐ and walk past a small picnic area overlooking the foot of the lake. Steps at the far end climb to a walled track, which to the left runs by a small quarry and on above the reservoir.

The track existed before the valley was flooded and, after a while, its course dips into the water. The path, however, shifts right, shortly dropping steeply down a flight of steps to cross a stream. Rising beyond, the way soon rejoins the old track, which now winds up the hill to a fork above the head of Digley Reservoir. The small lake above Digley is the Bilberry Reservoir, the dam of which failed after unusually heavy rains in 1852, just 12 years after it was completed and flooded the narrow valley below claiming 81 lives.

Take the right branch, eventually climbing to a junction and there go left,

contouring the valley side above Marsden Clough. In less than ½ mile, and not far after a gate, look for a path waymarked off on the right Ⓑ. Over a fence stile it rises as an abandoned green way, Old Lane, which soon curves to join a higher track dropping from the main road. The dilapidated track is succumbing to the reed tussock that blights the moor, but the extra height it gives repays the effort of passage by opening splendid views back down the Holme Valley and across to the moorland expanses of Holme Moss and Black Hill.

Follow the track up the valley, staying with it as it later swings back around a sharp bend. Continue for a further 50 yds to find a wall stile beside a gate on the right Ⓒ. Accompany the wall downfield, scaling another stile at the bottom from which a grass track drops to a bridge spanning the stream at the head of Marsden Clough. Climbing beyond, the track soon veers away to

The Digley Reservoir

cross the spur of moorland called Good Bent.

Ahead, peeping over the skyline is the Holme Moss transmitter mast, which at 750 feet (229m) high is a landmark from much of the northern Peakland high ground. It is the second mast to occupy the site, the original being put up in 1951 to broadcast BBC television. ITV did not appear until 1956 and for Yorkshire, was sent out from Emley Moor 8 miles away to the north east rather than here. By 1985, a second

mast had been erected alongside to broadcast VHF radio and, more lately, digital radio as well. It is one of the most powerful VHF transmitters in the country and its exceptional height (the base of the mast is already 1,720 feet (524m) above sea level) enables an unrivalled area of coverage.

Broaching the crest, the path bends above Hey Clough and makes for the brooding bulk of Black Hill. Eventually passing a solitary stone gate post **D**, the path dips across the stream and

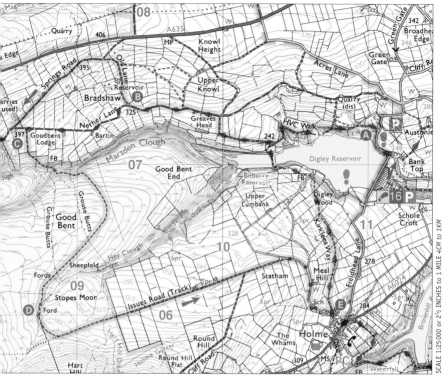

SCALE 1:25000 or 2½ INCHES to 1 MILE 4CM to 1KM

```
0    200   400   600   800 METRES   1
|----|----|----|----|----| KILOMETRES
0    200   400   600 YARDS         ½   MILES
```

continues briefly above the opposite bank before curving back towards the geometric enclosures, seen earlier from the top of Good Bent.

Through a gate, the way continues easily as a broad drove between the walled fields, running dead straight for nearly ³⁄₄ mile. Tracks join first from the right and then the left before the drove curves in steepening descent past a row of stone cottages and then the village school. Remaining with the lane will take you into Holme, where you will find the village pub, the **Fleece Inn**, just along to the right. The way back, however, lies along a waymarked track, which leaves through a gate on the left beside a barn, 100 yds beyond the school **E**.

Entering a field at the end, bear right to a stile in the far, lower corner and carry on beside the wall at the bottom of the next field as the Digley Reservoir comes into view. A guiding trod leads on over a succession of stiles, eventually intercepting a gravel path above the lake's southern shore. To the right it leads back to the car park. ●

Nether Lane

Black Moss and Butterley Reservoir

		GPS waypoints	
Start	Marsden		SE 047 118
Distance	6¼ miles (10.1km)	**A**	SE 043 109
Height gain	1,080 feet (329m)	**B**	SE 026 094
Approximate time	3 hours	**C**	SE 052 088
Parking	Standedge Visitor Centre car park by Marsden station	**D**	SE 048 107
Route terrain	Good moorland paths, *take care in mist*		
Ordnance Survey maps	Landranger 110 (Sheffield & Huddersfield), Explorer OL1 (The Peak District – Dark Peak area)		

Two main tributary valleys come together at Marsden to feed the River Colne, that flows from the south having its highest source at 1,670 feet (509m) on Wessenden Moor. Although not venturing quite that far, the route climbs to the Black Moss watershed for a glimpse into old Lancashire before dropping back to the town past a string of reservoirs in the Wessenden Valley.

The highest settlement in the Colne Valley, Marsden grew beside a network of packhorse routes and a coach road crossing the Pennines between Huddersfield and Manchester, which was built in 1760 by Blind Jack Metcalfe of Knaresborough. Within 80 years, canal and railway followed, transforming the place from a tiny hamlet into a booming industrial town. The cottagers abandoned their hand-looms to work in the mills and iron works, of which at one time there were 30 crowded into the constricted valley. The prosperity provided money for the large church dedicated to St Bartholomew, built in 1895 to replace an earlier chapel that had stood across the road. There were other public buildings too, including a Mechanics Institute, where the working men sought to better themselves by education. Restored and still used for adult education and community events, its distinctive clock tower rises as a landmark above the town's roofs.

Leaving the car park facing **The Railway** pub, walk down Station Road and bear right over a bridge and past St Bartholomew's Church. Keep right along Towngate, cross the main road and continue up Old Mount Road opposite, which climbs steeply out of the town. Leaving the cottages behind, the view opens across the foot of the Wessenden Valley, where the high dam of the Butterley Reservoir is a prominent feature. After almost ½ mile, the gradient eases by a cluster of cottages. Look for a narrow footpath **A** signed off between them (not the track doubling back just before), which rises to the open hillside behind. Carry on beside a wall, passing through a gate at the top onto a higher track. Follow it left, rejoining the lane and walking a few yards further to a second junction.

Cross to a narrow path opposite, which drops awkwardly to cross a brook. Gaining height out of the gully, the path broadens and strikes south west across the moor. Over to the right is Pule Hill, its flanks pocked and scarred by stone quarries, while ahead

the Redbrook Reservoir shortly comes into sight. After $3/4$ mile of easy walking the path dips to ford a stream. Ascend to the track above where you will find a prominent marker stone just to the left **B**.

There, go right and re-cross the stream, climbing away across the moor on a good, slabbed path. Passing through a kissing-gate, the tussock yields to heather, which rises to a second fence just beyond the skyline. Although hardly a prominent hill, the

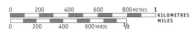

Marsden from Clark Hill

panorama is extensive. Behind is the long ridge of Standedge overlooking the mill towns of eastern Lancashire, while ahead, some 5 miles (8km) distant is the Holme Moss transmitter, broadcasting radio to much of Yorkshire. Leaving the top the way falls to a diminutive body of water, the Black Moss Reservoir.

Approaching the low dam, swing left beside the reservoir, which curiously straddles the watershed and has a retaining wall at either end. Drawing level with its eastern wall, turn right across the bund and a footbridge. Curving left, the continuing path wanders past the neighbouring Swellands Reservoir over the undulating moor. The way gradually falls beside the deepening rift of Blakely Clough, bringing the high dam of the Wessenden Reservoir into view. After descending more steeply, the path fords the stream just below a weir. A broader track carries on along the opposite flank, ending by a small, covered cistern from which there is a superb vista along the Wessenden Valley **C**.

A narrow path drops steeply to a bridge spanning Wessenden Brook. *You can then either climb to the service track and follow that down the valley or, alternatively, continue beside the brook and along the shore of Blakeley Reservoir, joining the track later beside the dam.* Carry on past the Butterley Reservoir to meet a lane.

A few yards to the left **D**, look for a path descending a long flight of steps to a turning area by garages and a house. Bear right to leave along a track, which soon runs between the tall buildings of one of the many mills that brought Victorian prosperity to the town. Emerging past a terrace of cottages walk left and continue ahead over a roundabout junction along Fall Lane. Approaching the main road, branch off left to pass beneath a bridge. Keep left again into Towngate and retrace your outward steps past the church to the car park.

Marsden's wealth was founded on wool, the fast-flowing streams coursing off the moors powering textile mills along the valley. As the industrial age gathered pace, many expanded and were converted to steam, fuelled by coal brought in along the canal and then by the railway. In the town, Enoch and James Taylor turned their blacksmith trade to making cropping frames, which were used to finish the cloth. However, the mechanising revolution was not a bloodless affair, and there was plenty of opposition to the new-fangled factory machinery that took the work out of the cottages. The Luddites attacked many of the new mills in Lancashire and Yorkshire, smashing the machines to the cry 'Enoch makes 'em and Enoch breaks 'em', alluding to the fact that his firm also made the sledgehammers wielded by the destructive gangs. ●

Castleton and Mam Tor

		GPS waypoints	
Start	Castleton		
Distance	6¼ miles (10.1km)	📷	SK 149 829
Height gain	1,325 feet (404m)	Ⓐ	SK 150 827
Approximate time	3 hours	Ⓑ	SK 135 813
		Ⓒ	SK 125 814
Parking	Car park at western edge of town – Pay and Display	Ⓓ	SK 126 826
		Ⓔ	SK 125 833
Route terrain	Generally clear upland paths and tracks	Ⓕ	SK 136 845
Ordnance Survey maps	Landranger 110 (Sheffield & Huddersfield), Explorer OL1 (The Peak District – Dark Peak area)		

Castleton occupies an enviable position near the head of the Hope Valley, dominated by the ruins of Peveril Castle and surrounded by bold hills and rolling moors. The walk begins with a long, steady ascent of Cave Dale to the gently undulating stone-walled fields above. There is then a sharp but short pull onto the 1,695ft (517m) summit of Mam Tor, which begins one of the finest scenic ridge walks in the Peak District. Linger to enjoy the views into the Vale of Edale and the Hope Valley, but save enough time to visit one of the nearby caves or perhaps, despite the daunting-looking climb, explore the castle ruins.

Surrounded by fantastic scenery and a multitude of attractions, it is little wonder that Castleton has become one of the principal tourist centres of the Peak District. The town grew up around the foot of Peveril Castle, which was founded in the late 11th century by William Peverel, an illegitimate son of William the Conqueror. The stronghold occupies a virtually impregnable position, with steep cliffs on three sides. It seems likely that initially a curtain wall was constructed only on the north side overlooking the town and that the other flanks relied on the natural defence afforded by the cliffs. The castle's most outstanding feature is the great keep, built by Henry II in 1176 after it had been forfeited to the Crown.

But it was not solely a defensive fortress, as it also served as a hunting lodge for the Royal Forest of the Peak before falling into disuse and subsequent ruin in the 15th century.

The predominant building in the village itself is the church, which, though mainly a 19th-century restoration, retains its fine Norman chancel arch. However, the sites drawing the greatest number of visitors to Castleton are the varied and spectacular caverns that honeycomb the surrounding hills. They are, in fact a mixture of natural caves and man-made tunnels, created as a result of mining for lead and other minerals. There are four show caves to choose from: the Peak, Blue John, Treak Cliff and Speedwell Caverns, the latter

Heading down to Hollins Cross

being particularly exciting as it involves a subterranean boat trip.

✏ After wandering around the exhibitions in the Castleton Centre beside the car park, follow the main street through the town as far as a sharp left-hand bend. Peak Cavern and Peveril Castle are signed off to the right, the road taking you past the church to a green in the middle of the old market place. Take the lane to the left at the top, but almost immediately, look for a bridleway to Cave Dale leaving between cottages on the right Ⓐ.

The path, sandwiched between abrupt rocky portals, winds up the narrow gorge, passing below the ruins of Peveril Castle perched high on the lip above. Beyond a gate at the head of the gorge, the way continues more easily through the upper part of the dale, eventually turning through a gate in the right-hand wall. Carry on to another gate and then at a waymark just beyond, bear left over the crest of the field, where the view right is to Mam Tor, the ramparts and ditches of its Iron Age summit fort evident even from here. Closer to hand, the landscape is pockmarked with the tips of old lead mines, which often broke through to the natural caves below. Pass through a gated sheep pen in the far corner to emerge onto a broad track Ⓑ.

Go right through a gate and, when you shortly reach a fork, take the track ahead. Carry on for almost another $^1/_2$ mile to the far side of the second large field. Ignore the gate ahead and instead mount a stile on the right Ⓒ.

Follow the left-hand wall away past grass-covered mounds that betray more abandoned workings. Mam Tor, now seen in front of you, is known as the 'Shivering Mountain' on account of instability in its lower layers of loose, soft shales, which are constantly crumbling and falling, giving the impression that the hill is moving or shivering. A landslide some years ago led to the closure of the A625 Sheffield to Chapel-en-le-Frith road and light traffic is now diverted through Winnats Pass, a steep and narrow route between towering limestone cliffs. Over a couple of stiles the onward way then falls gently downhill, leading to a gate onto a lane near the head of Winnats Pass Ⓓ.

Cross diagonally right to a gate (not the one directly opposite) and follow a field track that shortly meets another road. Through a small gate opposite, a path rises enthusiastically ahead up the grassy hill, culminating in steps onto the Edale road Ⓔ.

Instead of following the road, go through a gate on the right from which a stepped path takes you to the summit of Mam Tor. The views from the top are magnificent: to the north is the Vale of Edale from which the Pennine Way can be seen clearly snaking up onto Kinder Scout, and to the east you can just spot Peveril Castle above Castleton, with the Hope Valley winding between the hills beyond. The onward route lies ahead, an exhilarating ridge walk along the spine of the hill, overlooking a patch-

work of hedged green fields speckled with trees, while scattered across the hillside are lonely farmsteads and cottages. The path gently loses height for ³/₄ mile before reaching Hollins Cross, a junction of ancient paths marked by a stone cairn **F**.

Although the ridge path continues on to Lose Hill (alternatively known as Ward's Piece after a Sheffield man,

G. H. B. Ward, who made a major contribution to the cause of rambling in the area), we now leave it, branching off right to drop across the steep hillside in the direction of Castleton. Initially paved, it descends over stiles, eventually joining a sunken path that ends at a farm track. Follow it ahead, keeping right where it later forks to pass an outdoor centre. Beyond there a lane leads to the town. Go forward when you meet the main road, bending right with it through the centre to return to the car park. ●

Langsett and Midhope Reservoirs

Langsett and Midhope Reservoirs

		GPS waypoints
Start	Langsett Reservoir	⬚ SE 210 004
Distance	6½ miles (10.5km)	Ⓐ SE 215 001
Height gain	950 feet (290m)	Ⓑ SK 225 997
Approximate time	3 hours	Ⓒ SK 233 986
Parking	Car park at start	Ⓓ SK 213 995
Route terrain	Generally good paths and tracks, quiet lanes	Ⓔ SE 197 000
		Ⓕ SE 197 006
Ordnance Survey maps	Landranger 110 (Sheffield & Huddersfield), Explorer OL1 (The Peak District – Dark Peak area)	

The Langsett Reservoir is a popular beauty spot and a favourite walk combines the lakeside woods with a return across the moorland flanks of Hingcliff Hill past the ruin of North America Farm. The route suggested here extends it to include a circuit of the adjacent but less-frequented Midhope Reservoir, and gives an opportunity to stride out along a quiet back lane.

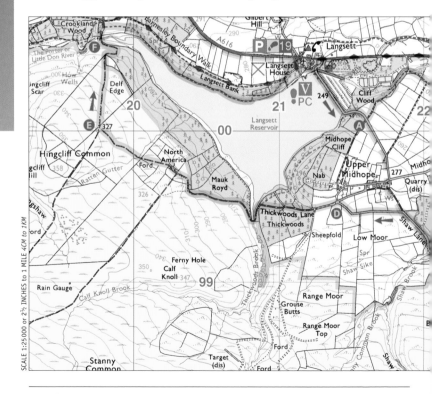

Like many of the Pennine reservoirs, Langsett and Midhope are a direct product of the Industrial Revolution, which spawned a dramatic growth of towns as people came off the land in droves to work in the mills and factories. Together with a treatment plant, both were built to supply water to Sheffield and Barnsley. Langsett, the larger of the two, was begun in 1889 and took almost six years to complete, with Midhope being finished just a little earlier. They exhibit the bold architecture of the time, when public buildings and other works were designed, not only to be functional, but also to emphasise the success and greatness of Empire and the Victorian era. The woods surrounding the reservoirs were a later feature, planted to help stabilise the banks as well as provide a cash crop in the timber they produced. Equally

Descending Hingcliff Hill

important today is their environmental benefit in providing habitats that encourage wildlife, a role that has been helped by more recent replanting using a variety of species.

Leave the car park past the barn and toilet facilities, winding between the stone cottages beyond to emerge onto the main road by the 19th-century **Waggon and Horses**. Go right and right again along a lane signed to Strines and the Derwent Valley. After crossing the Langsett Dam, follow the lane for another 150 yds to find a track on the right and a waymarked stile on the left **A**.

*The track offers a shortcut through the plantation of Upper Midhope to point **D**, missing out the Midhope Reservoir.* The main route, however, lies over the stile on the left. Head downfield, continuing beyond, by a wall on the left, for a further 150 yds to reach a stone stile. The path slants down through the adjacent woodland strip to run above the Little Don River.

Leave the wood over a stile by a bridge and keep ahead on this bank along a green track. Parting company with the water, it rises to a gate. Carry on at the edge of a field and then a more open area before joining a walled

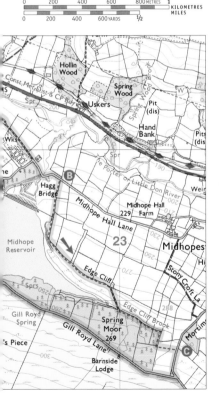

track that leads out to the bend of a lane. Follow it ahead across the outflow of the Midhope Reservoir, climbing beyond for 100 yds to reach a stile in the wall above **B**.

Head up the field edge and, drawing level with the Midhope dam, pass through a small gate to continue through a larch plantation fringing the water, not identified on the Ordnance Survey Explorer map. A fence later forces the path in an oblique descent to the valley where it then turns from the head of the lake to follow a stream. Watch for the path eventually swinging right and left before leaving the woodland onto a lane **C**.

Go right to a junction and then right again, the way signed to Upper Midhope and Langsett. The lane runs back above the trees bordering the southern shore of the lake, dipping after one mile across Shaw Brook, the main catchment stream for the reservoir. Shortly the lane swings left, rising to a sharp right-hand bend and junction of tracks **D**.

Take the concrete track off left, keeping ahead at its end through a gate into Thickwoods. Roughly paved, a relic

The Porter or Little Don River

of its wartime use to train tank crews in the run up to the D-Day landings, the track inconsiderately gives up the height you have so far gained, dropping to an inlet where Thickwoods Brook enters the Langsett Reservoir. After winding back to cross the stream climb away from the lake above Mauk Royd Wood, eventually passing through a gate onto the upper moor. Carry on past the evocative ruins of North America Farm, whose standing doorjambs are reminiscent of a prehistoric henge. It was one of several in the valley that were cleared when the reservoir was built to ensure the purity of the water. The gradient now eases as the path meanders across Hingcliff Common, topping out at a junction of paths **E**.

The path to the right falls towards the head of the Langsett Reservoir, twisting lower down to mollify the final steepness as it drops to a bridge across the Little Don River **F**. Climb away on a broad path, leaving after the initial pull along a gravelled, waymarked path on the right. It weaves easily through the trees above the full length of the lake. Fragmenting at the far end, the middle branch takes you directly back up to the car park. ●

Lose Hill

		GPS waypoints
Start	Edale	🖉 SK 123 853
Distance	6 miles (9.7km)	Ⓐ SK 123 852
Height gain	1,650 feet (503m)	Ⓑ SK 125 833
Approximate time	3½ hours	Ⓒ SK 136 845
Parking	Car park below village – Pay and Display	Ⓓ SK 153 853
		Ⓔ SK 143 848
Route terrain	Generally good upland paths	
Ordnance Survey maps	Landranger 110 (Sheffield & Huddersfield), Explorer OL1 (The Peak District – Dark Peak area)	

The long ridge of high ground separating the Vale of Edale from Castleton nestling at the head of the Hope Valley is one of the classic walks of the Peak District and provides stunning views almost every step of the way. It is here begun from the village of Edale and can be combined with Walk 10 over Lord's Seat to create a challenging exploration of the complete ridge.

🖉 From the Edale car park, follow the main lane to the right. Just beyond the de-restriction sign, a track Ⓐ to Hardenclough Farm and signed as a footpath to Castleton takes you across the River Noe. As the ground rises the eye is drawn towards the steep northern flank of Mam Tor, and the full line of the day's walk can be traced along the ridge to Lose Hill. The scene is equally absorbing to the right, where a great amphitheatre of high ground defines the head of the Edale Valley.

Beyond Hardenclough Farm, the track swings across a boisterous stream and rises energetically to the next farm, Greenlands. Just before its private entrance, leave through a bridle gate on the left. Take the path to the right, which is signed Mam Tor and gains height across the steep flank of the hill. A final pull leads to the high pass of Mam Nick, joining the lane for the last few yards to the top. Through a gate on

the left Ⓑ, a good path doubles back onto the summit of Mam Tor. Along the way are set reminders of the people who constructed the prehistoric fort on its top; a piece of pottery, an iron torque, a plough and depictions of dwellings.

On a clear day, the panorama from the top is superb; Kinder and the flat-topped, high moorland of the Dark Peak lie to the north, while along the valley beyond Castleton lies a very different landscape of grassy limestone hills. Particularly striking are Winnats Pass and Cave Dale, deep gorges cutting back into the steep slope of the main valley behind the town.

Mam Tor's commanding position above two adjacent valleys proclaimed status for the Bronze Age people who came here to bury their tribal leaders some 3,500 years ago. Some time later, a village grew around the ceremonial site and the flattened platforms of around 100 dwellings and store huts

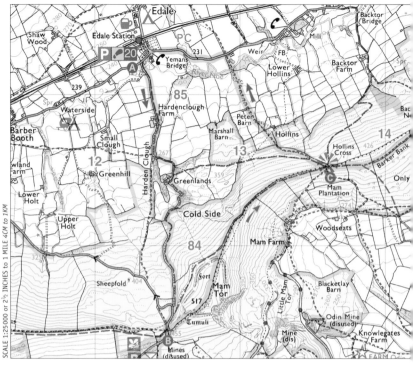

dotted around the summit can still be seen. The most impressive man-made feature is the ditch and rampart defence of an Iron Age hill fort, which would, in its day, have been even more imposing, topped with a high wooden palisade and later a stone wall. Much, however, is still to be learned about this intriguing site, which is the second highest known hill fort in Britain.

After the strenuous ascent from Edale, the next leg of the route appears positively inviting. Beginning with an attenuated, gradual fall to the shallow saddle of Hollins Cross **C**, it continues over Back Tor to Lose Hill at the far end of the long ridge, still some 2 miles distant. The path sticks to the top of the narrow spine almost all the way and affords a splendid view on either side. Approaching the foot of the craggy northern face of Back Tor, the way slips over a stile on the left and clambers up

a good path beside the cliff. After admiring the view from the top of the rocky precipice, and perhaps adding to the efforts of the pebble artists on the nearby cairn, continue along the final stretch to Lose Hill **D**.

There is nothing remarkable about the top of the hill except, of course, the view, which is celebrated in a topograph naming seemingly just about everything for miles around. Prominent across the mouth of the Noe Valley is Win Hill, its summit cone looking something of an afterthought to finish off the job. Since the middle of the 20th century, Lose Hill has acquired another name, Ward's Piece, bestowed to honour G. H. B. Ward. Among many other causes he was a leading activist in the fight for public access to the moors during the early 20th century. Ward founded the Sheffield Clarion Ramblers in 1900, the first club of its type for working class people and was involved with several other footpath societies, as well as the Ramblers' Association and

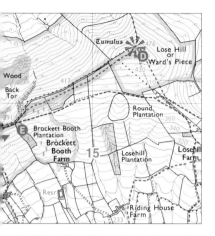

the Youth Hostel Association. It was the Ramblers' Association who bought Lose Hill for him in 1945, which he then generously presented to the National Trust.

Although surrounded by access land on its upper slopes, there is no way off the hill into the Edale Valley. You can drop off south to either Hope or Castleton, both quite acceptable routes, but it is then a long walk back to Edale. The sensible choice is to retrace your steps along the ridge, where you will find the views revealed in a completely new light. Particularly impressive is the massive ongoing slump on the eastern face of Mam Tor, that in 1979 finally

Hollins Cross and Mam Tor

took with it the main road out of Castleton to the west.

Returning to the stile at the foot of Back Tor ⓔ*, you then have a choice of routes. Immediately before the stile, a path descends fairly steeply off the hill. Lower down, it joins a track through the intake wall, which leads past Backtor Farm out to the lane. Alternatively, you may wish to hang on to your hard-won height for a little longer, in which case, stick with the ridge path until you reach Hollins Cross* ⓒ*.* Bear right there and then take the lower branch where it shortly splits, the path heading towards Grindslow Knoll, the prominent hill above Edale on the opposite side of the valley. Through a gate at the bottom, drop to a track from Hollins Farm, which also takes you to the lane. Edale and the car park lie to the left.

Hollins Cross stands on a high pass at a junction of ancient paths, one of which was a medieval coffin route along which mourners from Edale carried their dead across the hill for burial at the parish church in Castleton. With the arrival of the industrial age, the direction of passage across the hill was reversed as people from Castleton trudged across to work in Edale's textile mill. ●

Crowden and Millstone Rocks

		GPS waypoints
Start	Crowden	
Distance	6½ miles (10.5km)	SK 072 992
Height gain	1,550 feet (472m)	Ⓐ SK 060 986
Approximate time	3½ hours	Ⓑ SK 055 981
Parking	Car park at start	Ⓒ SK 044 979
Route terrain	Good tracks beside reservoir, clear but peaty upland paths, *take care in mist*	Ⓓ SK 044 992
		Ⓔ SK 067 995
Ordnance Survey maps	Landranger 110 (Sheffield & Huddersfield), Explorer OL1 (The Peak District – Dark Peak area)	

Once part of a royal hunting forest, Longdendale now cradles a chain of reservoirs that stretches for more than 5½ miles (8.9km). This superb walk follows the two middle lakes and then climbs back above the valley to the spectacular vantage of Millstone Rocks, which looks out across Longdendale and its southern escarpments to the moorland expanse of Bleaklow. The return is no less dramatic, with glimpses into the twin valleys of Crowden Brook.

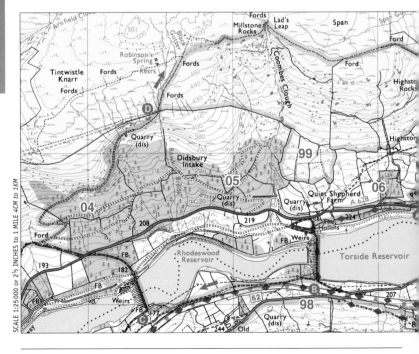

SCALE 1:25000 or 2½ INCHES to 1 MILE 4CM to 1KM

🥾 Leave the far end of the car park towards the toilets, there turning right on a path beside the campsite, which leads to a junction at the entrance to a farm. Through a gate to the left, a track leads past the farm and over a bridge spanning crowden brook. The two arms of the stream cleave deep valleys that bite into the lonely upland moors, which rise to Black Hill, one of the highest points of the Peak. The onward track then begins to climb, cresting the rise beside a plantation of pine. Falling beyond, a view opens across the Torside Reservoir along whose far bank once ran the Sheffield, Ashton under Lyne & Manchester Railway. Plainly visible is the embankment, which took it across the foot of Torside Clough, a deep cleft in the escarpment along which the Pennine Way is routed off Bleaklow Head.

The Woodhead railway between Manchester and Sheffield was the first to be pushed across the Pennines and opened in 1845. The tunnel, upon which the line depended, took almost eight years to complete and, at just over 3 miles, was then one of the world's longest. The enterprise was an immediate success and within seven years a second tunnel enabling two-way working was opened to accommodate increasing traffic. At one point around 500 steam trains a day were passing through. However, steep gradients and smoke pollution within the tunnels were continuing problems. Work began on electrification in 1936, but was disrupted by the war. It also became clear that the existing tunnels were too small and could not be adapted to carry the overhead wires. In consequence, a third tunnel, this time two-way, was dug. It saw its first trains in 1953 and remained in use until the line was closed in 1981. They are now owned by the National Grid, who use one of the Victorian tunnels to take the trans-Pennine power cables beneath the summit, thus protecting them from the severe winter weather on the tops. The cables are shortly due for replacement and it was planned to re-lay them through the 'new' tunnel. However, there is pressure to re-open the route to carry freight and help alleviate trans-Pennine road traffic, and at the moment, its future remains uncertain.

Reaching the main road Ⓐ, cross to a path opposite, which descends right to meander through a strip of plantation above the lake. Through a gate at the far end of the wood, drop to cross a service track and continue down steps to another track below. Follow it across the top of the Torside Dam to find a waymarked dirt track leaving through a gate on the right Ⓑ. Running below the course of the railway, it soon emerges from trees to give a view along Rhodeswood Reservoir, unfortunately compromised by striding pylons carrying one of the main trans-Pennine

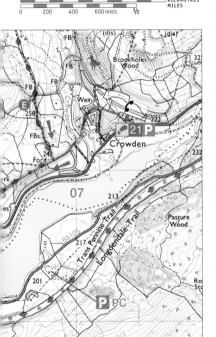

Past Crowden Quarries to Woodhead

electricity supplies. At a fork beyond a stile, bear right, the way losing height to the dam at the foot of the lake .

Walk back to the northern bank and carry on up the service drive to the main road. Through a gate opposite, follow a rough track onto the heather-clad hillside. Stay with it around a sharp right bend and then keep left at a fork. Later bend left, pass another junction and then bend sharp right. Continue to a stile and gate into the upper part of the Didsbury Intake plantation. The track pursues its rising plod through the trees, eventually levelling below the cliffs of an old quarry. Where the track ends, carry on along a path, climbing across the fractured face before eventually turning up to reach a stile at the top beside the peaty runnel of Rawkins Brook .

Crossing the stream, pick up a rough path that strikes north east across the moss towards the higher ground, some ¼ mile distant. Wet weather might sometimes have you casting around for firm going, but in late summer the purple expanse of flowering heather is more than ample compensation. The way rises to the top of an outcrop, Millstone Rocks, which stands above the impressive rocky amphitheatre of Coombes Clough.

The path, now improved underfoot initially follows the rim, before turning in above the ravine to guide you to a convenient crossing point. Clambering away at the far side the path drifts back from the edge as it begins a gradual descent across the moor. Over to the left, peeping above the horizon is the mast of the Holme Moss transmitter, rather deceptively only 4 miles away. As the intermediate ground falls away, the view opens to the twin valleys of Crowden Brook, which find their source on the bleak upper slopes of Black Hill. Beyond the end of a broken wall, the route falls along a shallow trough then accompanies another wall down the hill. Ahead, extensive quarries high on the abrupt nose of Hey Moss overlook the foot of the Woodhead Reservoir, the highest of the series that cascade down the valley.

At the bottom corner of the wall, cross a stile and continue steeply down the hillside towards a farm, soon reaching a junction of paths beside a small memorial copse of trees . Turn through the small gate on the right and follow the boundary away across successive enclosures to emerge onto the track along which the walk began. Go left back to the car park. ●

Lantern Pike

		GPS waypoints	
Start	Hayfield	🖋	SK 036 869
Distance	7¼ miles (11.7km)	Ⓐ	SK 040 868
Height gain	1,400 feet (427m)	Ⓑ	SK 049 883
Approximate time	3½ hours	Ⓒ	SK 035 894
Parking	Car park at former railway station – Pay and Display	Ⓓ	SK 032 902
		Ⓔ	SK 029 904
Route terrain	Clear paths and tracks across moorland	Ⓕ	SK 023 895
		Ⓖ	SK 025 881
Ordnance Survey maps	Landranger 110 (Sheffield & Huddersfield), Explorer OL1 (The Peak District – Dark Peak area)	Ⓗ	SK 021 868

Nestling below the bleak upland of Kinder, Hayfield is the starting point for this grand circuit that encircles one of the head valleys of the River Sett. The prominent, local landmark of Lantern Pike offers expansive views before an easy valley return along the course of a disused railway.

Annual sheep dog trials, well dressing and a May Queen procession emphasise the village feel of Hayfield today. Yet during the 19th century, it had grown to a small but bustling town with the railway, which arrived in 1868, serving local industries such as textile mills and calico printing, paper-making and quarrying. Earlier, it had been a staging post on a packhorse trail across the hills, a fact remembered in the **Pack Horse Inn**, which has stood there since 1577. Many of the stone cottages date from the 17th century and were well-fenestrated in their upper storeys to admit light for weaving woollen cloth on hand-looms. More recently, Hayfield saw the birth of Arthur Lowe,

remembered for, among many other things, his role as Captain Mainwaring in the ever-popular *Dad's Army* television series. The television theme is continued in the higher valley at Little Hayfield, where Tony Warren creator of *Coronation Street* and Pat Phoenix (Elsie Tanner), one of its original, long-standing stars both lived.

Birch Vale Reservoir

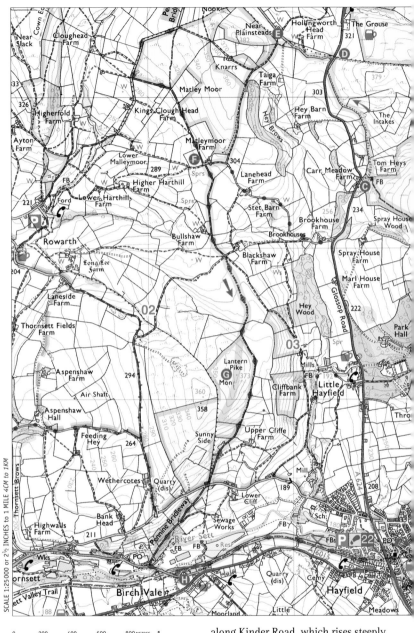

Begin from the car park at the former station and cross the main road at the traffic lights. Carry on beside the church into the town centre and go left over the River Sett. Just beyond, turn right into Bank Street and continue along Kinder Road, which rises steeply out of the town. After ¼ mile, as the gradient eases, look for a track signed off on the left to the **Snake Inn (A)**.

The gated, stony track winds determinedly up the hillside, later climbing past a clump of beech trees, conspicuous by their isolation. Out to the left across the valley is Lantern Pike, over

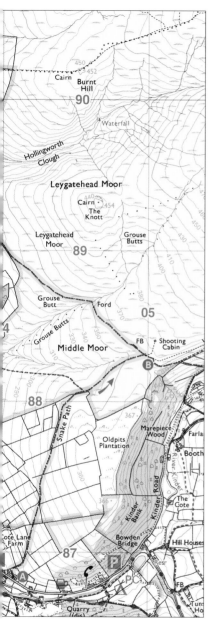

Take the left path, signed to Glossop via Carr Meadow, which, beyond a short causeway over boggy ground, winds carelessly across the heath. Later dip to ford a brook and continue around the flank of The Knott, from where there is a superb view along the Sett Valley. The path then gradually steepens towards Carr Meadows, dropping to bridge a stream in Hollingworth Clough and meeting a track coming from the road **C**.

Bearing right, climb at the edge of the open moor, taking the left branch when you reach a fork. The way now levels towards the head of the valley. Keep right where the path subsequently splits, continuing to a stile in the corner, which leads out to the road facing a junction **D**.

If you are ready for refreshment, the **Grouse Inn** lies a short way to the right, but the onward route lies along the lane opposite, signed towards Charlesworth. After $\frac{1}{4}$ mile, just beyond the crest of the rise, leave along a way-marked track on the left **E**. Reaching a junction, bear left and, through a gate at the end, carry on at the edge of coarse pasture. Remain by the wall to find a stile in the corner and walk down to a gravel track. Turning right soon brings you to a junction by Matleymoor Farm **F**.

Take the walled track to the left, which leads towards Blackshaw Farm. As the track swings into the yard, go through a field-gate on the right into a rough, open pasture. Strike a diagonal left from the corner, soon picking up a trod making for Lantern Pike. Joining a track at the far side, follow it right through a gate and up onto the access land. Just beyond the National Trust sign, bear off right to make a direct ascent of the hill. The strenuous pull leads to a topograph on the summit **G**.

The way continues above a low but none the less impressive escarpment

which the walk returns. Levelling, the path progresses onto the rougher, open moor and the National Trust access land. The scene opens ahead across the heather to Leygatehead Moor and farther right, the foreboding mass of Kinder Scout. Carry on for $\frac{1}{4}$ mile towards white-painted shooting cabins, to find a junction just before them **B**.

before descending to a wall. Turn left and follow it steeply down to regain the track you left earlier. To the right, through a gate, carry on down the hill, eventually emerging onto a narrow lane. Go briefly right past a row of one-time quarrymen's cottages before branching left along another downward track marked as the Pennine Bridleway to Hayfield. At a hairpin bend, keep ahead through a gate along an old, leafy way, which comes out beside mill cottages at Spinner Bottom below Birch Vale.

Turn left, crossing the River Sett to find, just past the **Special Touch Café**, a waymarked path leaving through a gate on the left . After a couple of twists it settles along the course of the former railway, heading up the valley above a large reservoir built to supply the mill. One mile's easy walking returns you to the car park. ●

On Lantern Pike

Hathersage

		GPS waypoints
Start	Hathersage	✐ SK 231 813
Distance	7¼ miles (11.7km)	Ⓐ SK 229 811
Height gain	1,400 feet (427m)	Ⓑ SK 233 806
Approximate time	3½ hours	Ⓒ SK 213 811
Parking	Car park in Oddfellows Road – Pay and Display	Ⓓ SK 221 817
		Ⓔ SK 225 823
Route terrain	Clear tracks and field paths, stepping stones across the River Derwent	Ⓕ SK 218 829
		Ⓖ SK 229 837
Dog friendly	Stepping stones may pose a problem for some dogs	
Ordnance Survey maps	Landranger 110 (Sheffield & Huddersfield), Explorer OL1 (The Peak District – Dark Peak area)	

In contrast to the high moorland, the Derwent Valley here is a mixture of green meadows, wooded valleys and rolling hills. The walk climbs for the views on both sides of the river before returning along the picturesque valley of Hood Brook. Note: Heavy rain can make the stepping stones across the River Derwent north of Offerton impassable and necessitate a riverside return to Leadmill Bridge to pick up the alternative route from Hathersage.

Today's picture of bright streets and attractive cottages is a far cry from the pall of 19th-century grime and smoke, when Hathersage's mills churned out millions of needles and pins. The village is, however, more famous for its literary connections, one real and the other legendary. Charlotte Brontë stayed here awhile, taking the name for her most famous heroine from tombs in the 14th-century church, Eyre. Little John, right-hand man of Robin Hood, is supposedly buried in the same graveyard, which is passed at the end of the walk.

✐ From the car park, follow Oddfellows Road to the right past the Memorial Hall and go left at the junction. Before reaching the railway, turn right into Dore Lane, continuing beyond the bridge to a bend in front of Nether Hall Lodge Ⓐ. Through a field-gate on the left, a farm track is signed away at the field edge to Leadmill Bridge. Emerging onto the road there, cross the bridge and immediately leave through a narrow gate on the right onto the riverbank Ⓑ.

Head upstream beside the Derwent. However, after 200 yds, bear left by a dilapidated barn to climb a wooded bank to a wall stile at the top. Follow the right-hand boundary into the next field, but where the wall later drops away, strike across to a gate onto a track below Mount Pleasant Farm. Pause to enjoy the view across to Stanage Edge and then take the track on the right towards Broadhay Farm.

Stepping across the Derwent

Straight after a bridge spanning Dunge Brook (a contraction of the old English 'dene ge' meaning valley district), leave through a gate on the left and walk upfield above the beck. Continue through another gate into Callow Wood, the ongoing path gaining height through the trees along the valley side. Eventually, pass out through a gate in the right-hand wall and bear left up the field to a stile. Just above is a gate into the yard of Callow House Farm.

Leave to the left, but then immediately cross a stile on the right to find a path doubling back above the former barns. Over another stile and stream, the obvious path continues across the hillside, shortly emerging onto a tarmac drive. To the right, it leads to Offerton Hall, one of seven large farmhouses in the area said to have been provided in the 14th century by Robert and Elizabeth Eyre for their seven sons. Nearing the hall, the way twists abruptly down hill, passing its entrance and then a neighbouring cottage. Just past there, leave the drive through a field-gate on the right **C**.

A contained path drops through the field and continues as a downhill trod to the River Derwent where, if, the water level permits, cross the stepping stones.

Otherwise, follow the riverbank downstream back to Leadmill Bridge. Retrace your steps to Nether Hall lodge **A***, but now take the lane opposite and at the end, go left to the main road. Cross and turn right to find a path signed off between the bank and an outdoor shop, which continues behind house gardens and beside a cricket field. Rejoining the stream, keep going to a bridge. Cross and strike a diagonal course over parkland to rise through Cliff Wood. Emerging above the trees,*

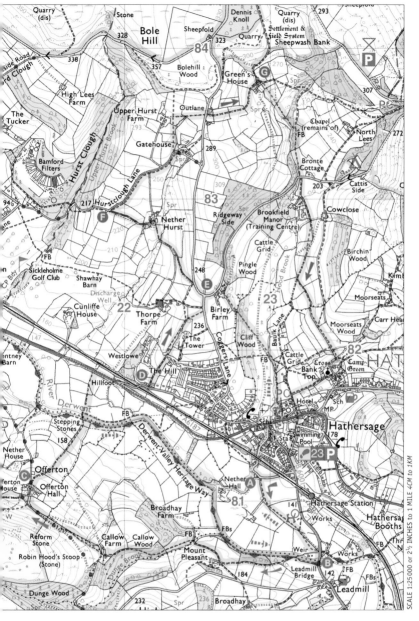

0	200	400	600	800 METRES	1
					KILOMETRES
					MILES
0	200	400	600 YARDS	½	

accompany a fence up to Birley Farm.
Over a stile behind the barns, go right
and then left, leaving through gates
onto a lane. Follow it left to a junction
E, there turning right to rejoin the
main route.

Assuming you made it across the
river, head directly away, passing
through gaps in old hedges to reach the
main road. Follow it right for 200 yds
then fork left up Hill Foot. A short
distance beyond the railway bridge,
look for a stepped path beside a cottage
on the left **D**.

Climb to a hand-gate and on up a

track. Where that swings right, cross the stile in front. Continue at the field edge to another stile and then keep right to a small gate. Now strike out across a final field to a squeeze gap onto a lane. Go left up the hill to a junction , there keeping left on Coggers Lane. In the 18th century Geer Green School stood in the adjacent field and was used by Charlotte Brontë as the model for Moreton School in her novel, *Jane Eyre*.

Carry on a further 150 yds then bear left through a gate into the corner of a field. Head out, with the trees of an old boundary on your right. Through a gate at the end, drop beside the left boundary to a stream at the bottom. Follow the ongoing hedge up to a gate, emerging at a junction of tracks by Nether Hurst. Take the one opposite, winding past a pond and bunkhouse. Where the track finishes, keep ahead on a sunken, hedged path, which leads to another old track, Hurstclough Lane.

Follow it or the adjacent field path right for almost ¹/₂ mile to a sharp right-hand bend, where there is a stile on the left. Climb beside a small stream, bearing right in the fourth field to find a stone stile in the corner. Strike across a final field to meet a lane opposite a house, Out Lane. Go right and then

Little John's Grave

quickly left along a track beside the buildings, which continues over a cattle-grid across the fields. It eventually wanders down to a large farm, Green's House, entering a narrow yard between the buildings. Immediately through a gate at the far side, slip through a gap in the right-hand wall.

Carry on down the fields towards a wood, dropping through the trees and over a bridge to continue beside Hood Brook. Emerging in a field, walk at the edge to reach a narrow lane.

Through a gate opposite, skirt Brookfield Manor and head across the field beyond. At a waymark in the middle, bear right along a track that continues across the next field. Through a gate at the far side, turn off to follow the hedge on the left. Over a stile and with the hedge now on your right, keep going in subsequent fields, the way cresting a low rise before falling to a stream. A stepped path scales the opposite bank; at the top of which go right to come out opposite the church. Walk left to enter the churchyard, where you will find Little John's grave opposite the south porch.

The band of Sherwood outlaws might be merely folk heroes, but when the burial here was opened in 1784, a huge thighbone was found, suggesting a man about 7ft (2.13m) tall.

Continue west past the church and extension cemetery, leaving at the far end along a descending path to a lane. Go left to the main road and cross to a foot-path between the buildings opposite. Joining a street, walk ahead back to the car park.

Edale and Jacob's Ladder

		GPS waypoints
Start	Edale	
Distance	8 miles (12.9km)	SK 123 853
Height gain	1,690 feet (515m)	Ⓐ SK 122 861
Approximate time	4 hours	Ⓑ SK 105 872
		Ⓒ SK 095 872
Parking	Car park below village – Pay and Display	Ⓓ SK 079 865
		Ⓔ SK 081 861
Route terrain	Moorland paths, easy scramble onto moor, *take care in mist*	Ⓕ SK 102 852
Ordnance Survey maps	Landranger 110 (Sheffield & Huddersfield), Explorer OL1 (The Peak District – Dark Peak area)	

This walk starts from the hamlet of Edale and rises gently at first, up the spectacular valley of Grindsbrook Clough and eventually scrambling out at the top onto the southern flank of the remote Kinder Scout plateau above the Vale of Edale. There are some splendid views and a sense of wilderness as the next stage skirts the head of the dale, passing some fantastically shaped gritstone boulders. After descending Jacob's Ladder there is an easy final stretch across the valley fields.

Strictly speaking, Edale is the name of a valley in which lie five distinct hamlets or booths, although in practice, the name has become identified with the main settlement, Grindsbrook Booth. To the north stretches the highest and wildest moorland of the Dark Peak and Edale has become a major walking centre. It is also the start (or finish) of the Pennine Way, which traverses some of England's remotest countryside on its 250-mile (400km) route to Kirk Yetholme in the Cheviot Hills on the Scottish border.

Leaving the car park by the toilets, go right beneath the railway and follow the lane to **The Old Nag's Head** at the top of the village. Beyond there, it degrades to a track leading to a stone lodge at the entrance of Grindslow House Ⓐ. Turn off there along a path on the right over a bridge, signed to Grindsbrook.

To the left a flagged path rises gently across an open hillside field, before long entering a pleasant wood. Emerging at the far side, cross a stream and continue up the narrowing valley, the way steadily becoming more rugged. Higher up, path and stream come together, the path eventually forced to pick a better line above the opposite bank. Where the valley then splits, keep with the left branch, scrambling on to emerge below a large cairn at the head of Grindsbrook Clough Ⓑ. Move left a few yards to pick up a slabbed path striking west, which crosses the shoulder of Grindslow Knoll to continue above the edge of Crowden Clough. You are following the perimeter of the vast expanse of Kinder Scout; a

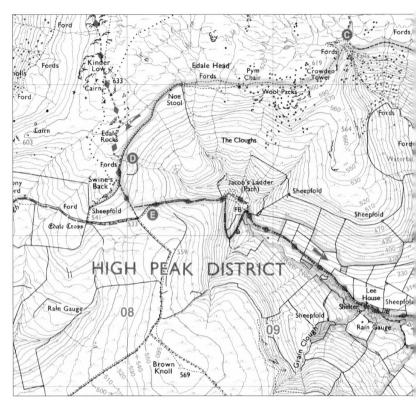

bleak, featureless waste furrowed by deep peat gullies known as groughs. The views to the south extend across the whole of the White Peak, the prominent hill to the east across the valley being Lose Hill. Intermittently paved, the way remains clear, eventually leading you to the head of Crowden Brook **C**.

Cross the brook below its tributary streams and climb towards a great buttress of rock, Crowden Tower. The way winds on past the ever-more fantastic gritstone rock formations of the Wool Packs and Pym Chair. Beyond, the going can be boggy as it crosses the gathering grounds of the River Noe to reach the last outcrop, Noe Stool. Curving around the head of the valley, stay below Edale Rocks to join the Pennine Way at a large cairn **D**. Walk ahead towards the distinctive knoll of Swine's Back, keeping with the paved

path as it then curves left to meet a track beside a stone wall **E**.

Follow it down to the left, shortly reaching a junction by a cairn. Either path will do, that to the left is short and steep, the one through the gate finds an easier line in an extended loop. Both lead to a narrow stone bridge across the infant Noe. Known as Jacob's Ladder, the path once formed part of a major packhorse route across the moors. From the bridge it is then easy walking along the valley to Lee Farm, the way becoming a metalled track as it approaches Upper Booth. Opposite a telephone box **F**, a fingerpost to Edale directs you left into the farmyard. Passing a barn go out right and then almost immediately left, turning right again after a few paces through a gate along a track, still signed to Edale. Beyond another gate, the way lies as an obvious trod across successive fields,

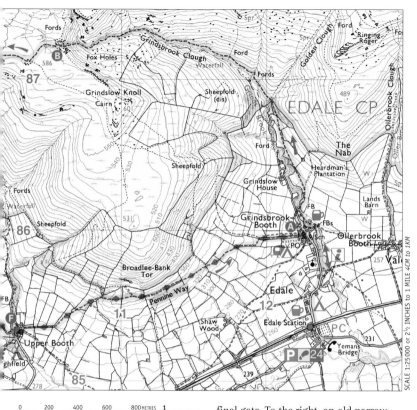

SCALE 1:25 000 or 2½ INCHES to 1 MILE 4CM to 1KM

0   200   400   600   800 METRES   **1**
                                   KILOMETRES
                                   MILES
0   200   400   600 YARDS   ½

shortly passing a ruined barn to a small gate. The main path winds on through an area of hummocky ground, crossing more fields before leaving through a final gate. To the right, an old narrow track bordered by hawthorn, ash and holly follows a stream back to the head of the village by **The Old Nag's Head**. Return along the lane to the car park. ●

Among Wool Packs

Win Hill and Hope Cross

		GPS waypoints
Start	Ashopton	🖉 SK 202 858
Distance	8¼ miles (13.3km)	Ⓐ SK 198 856
Height gain	1,590 feet (485m)	Ⓑ SK 193 851
Approximate time	4 hours	Ⓒ SK 186 850
Parking	Heatherdene car park	Ⓓ SK 161 874
Route terrain	Clear tracks and paths through forest and upland grazing	Ⓔ SK 163 878
Ordnance Survey maps	Landranger 110 (Sheffield & Huddersfield), Explorer OL1 (The Peak District – Dark Peak area)	

After an initial climb through forest plantations overlooking the Ladybower Dam to the craggy height of Win Hill, there follows a superb, view-filled saunter on a broad, grassy ridge over Wooler Knoll. Dropping into the Ashop Valley the return undulates along the full length of the western arm of the reservoir.

🖉 From the southern corner of the lower car park, follow a path past the toilets signed to the Ladybower Dam. Coming level with the dam, drop to the road, where there is a monument listing the worthies of the Water Board when the dam was opened by King George VI on 25 September 1945.

Although begun ten years earlier, the dam's construction had been hampered by the war and it was not completed until 1943, with a further two years being required for it to fill up. Unlike the dams higher up the valley, it is not built of solid masonry, but is a massive earthen embankment waterproofed with a clay core sat upon a concrete foundation that extends deep into the hills to prevent water seeping around the side. Fifty years of use inevitably took their toll and during the 1990s the dam underwent a major refurbishment. This included the provision of a pathway across the top of the 650-foot (594m) dam, which has opened new options for walks in the area, such as this one.

Follow the footpath across the dam, turning right along the bridleway on the far side. Abandon it after 200 yds for a rising path into the trees signed off to New Barn Ⓐ. The path heralds a steady ascent across the slope of the hill. Emerging through a gate onto a broader path, go left, the way still rising albeit more gently. Keep going for a good ½ mile, eventually meeting a path coming up along Parkin Clough Ⓑ. To the right, a stepped path makes a direct attack on the hillside, ending through a gate at another junction of paths.

Take the one diagonally opposite, signed to Win Hill, which climbs on through Winhill Plantation. Breaking cover, pass through a gap in a wall for the final pull onto the tor crowning Win Hill Ⓒ.

With the reservoirs below your feet and hills all around, the view is extensive. Across the water is the tor-studded line of Derwent Edge, while in the other direction across the Noe Valley is Lose Hill, otherwise known as

The Ladybower Reservoir from Winhill Pike

Ward's Piece, the culmination of a long ridge of hills dividing the Vale of Edale from the Hope Valley. As the walk unfolds, the eye is later drawn along Edale and to the high plateau of Kinder, overshadowing it from the north.

Having taken your fill of the panorama, drop to the path below the summit rocks and head west in a gentle descent. Eventually, as the accompanying boundary is left behind, the path arcs right and assumes the line of the ridge, re-opening the view across Ladybower before it closes with the plantation boundary beyond Wooler Knoll. Watch for the path later curving left to meet a lower track, the line of the Roman road linking two forts, Navio beside the River Noe and Melandra near Glossop. Passing through a gate, it runs for ¹/₂ mile to Hope Cross ⒟. The 18th-century waymark stands at a junction of ancient trails, its square crown indicating the direction and destination of each (notice the unusual rendering of 'Shefield').

Through the gate just beyond, immediately turn right over a stile into the forest. Bearing left, a dark path drops for ¹/₄ mile through the trees to emerge in a small clearing by the ruin of a building. Turn right (not sharp right) on a path falling steeply straight down the hill, winding at the bottom to meet a broad forest track at the head of the western arm of the Ladybower Reservoir ⒠. To the right, it undulates above the shore for 3 miles to return you to the dam at the foot of the lake.

The Ladybower Reservoir lies at the meeting of two of the Derwent's tributaries; the River Ashop, which has its source on the watershed of the Snake Pass, and the much smaller Ladybower Brook which tumbles from the east and gives the lake its name. When completed in 1943, the reservoir was the largest man-made body of water in Britain, extending over 242 acres (98 hectares). Ladybower was the third in the chain of reservoirs now filling the upper valley

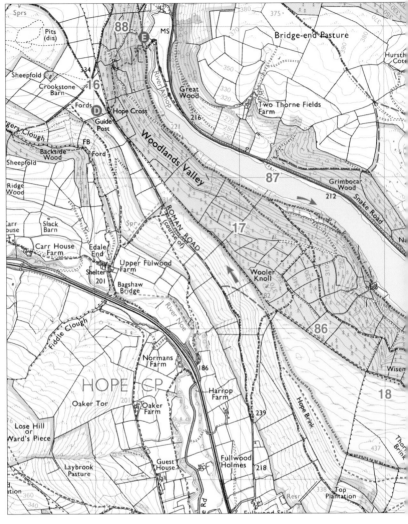

The Ladybower overflow

and followed the completion of the Howden and Derwent water supply reservoirs some 30 years earlier. The rising waters flooded two small villages; Derwent, part-way up the northern arm and Ashopton, which overlooked the confluence with the River Ashop. The villagers were re-housed and their cottages razed and even the dead were exhumed from Derwent's

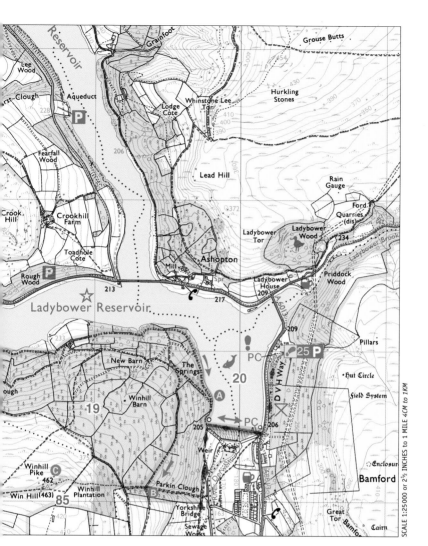

SCALE 1:25000 or 2½ INCHES to 1 MILE 4CM to 1KM

small churchyard for reburial in nearby Bamford. Only the church spire was left intact, an intended memorial to the village, but by 1947 that too had been demolished.

The Ladybower Reservoir was built, not only to extend the water supply capability of the area, but also to help maintain a consistent flow in the River Derwent below the dam. When river levels drop, water is released from the reservoir to protect the environment and wildlife dependent upon it. One, or perhaps two, unusual features are the circular, bell-mouth shafts located at either side near the foot of the lake. They act as giant plug holes to prevent the reservoir overflowing and channel the excess water into the River Derwent at the base of the dam. The reservoirs collectively hold some 10.5 billion gallons (47.8 million cubic metres) of water and satisfy around 10% of the East Midlands' needs, supplying water to the cities and surrounding areas of Derby, Leicester, Nottingham and Sheffield.

Marsden and Standedge

		GPS waypoints
Start	Marsden	
Distance	8½ miles (13.7km)	🖉 SE 047 118
Height gain	1,300 feet (396m)	Ⓐ SE 040 119
		Ⓑ SE 030 122
Approximate time	4 hours	Ⓒ SE 002 122
Parking	Standedge Visitor Centre car park by Marsden station	Ⓓ SE 018 094
		Ⓔ SE 037 101
Route terrain	Clear moorland paths, *take care in mist*	
Ordnance Survey maps	Landranger 110 (Sheffield & Huddersfield), Explorer OL1 (The Peak District – Dark Peak area)	

Where does the Peak District end and the South Pennines begin? This is an impossible question to answer as the two merge imperceptibly into each other. But it must happen somewhere near Marsden, for here on the northern fringes of the Peak District National Park, the towns and the scenery are unmistakably 'Pennine' in atmosphere and appearance. This ramble is mostly across open, bare moorland, bleak perhaps, but impressive and characterised by sweeping and uninterrupted vistas. There are no steep climbs and the lonely paths are clear on the ground, but choose a fine day to best enjoy the views.

Standedge

🖉 Emerging from the car park entrance beside the railway station, turn right and join the towpath of the Huddersfield Narrow Canal. Walk with the water on your right for a little less than ½ mile then cross using a footbridge Ⓐ, just short of the north-eastern portal of the Standedge Tunnel. The building by the tunnel mouth houses a **café**, while over to the right in a former warehouse is a small exhibition detailing the history of the tunnel.

At just over 3 miles, this is the longest (and highest) canal tunnel in Britain and was completed in 1811, linking the Calder Navigation to the Manchester and Cheshire waterways. Traffic declined during the early 20th century and it eventually closed in 1944, but was restored and re-opened again in 2001. Narrowboats once more pass beneath the Pennines, but in the old days, with no towpath for the horses, those on narrowboats had to 'leg' their boats through.

Climb up the lane from the canal to a junction opposite the Tunnel End Inn and go left along Waters Road. Keep walking for $\frac{1}{2}$ mile, passing the entrance to Hey Green to reach Eastergate Cottage, just a little farther on Ⓑ.

Leave the lane there, forking left onto a waymarked path that follows Redbrook Clough to Close Gate Bridge, an ancient packhorse bridge overlooking the confluence of two streams. Cross and turn right, walking up for 100 yds before bearing left into a narrower grassy side valley. Look out for a large slab of rock bearing the fossilised fronds of a tree. Curving across the head of another stream, the path breaks out across the open moor, the gently rising way marked by occasional gritstone posts, which identified the old packhorse trail. It eventually meets the Pennine Way below a small parking area beside the main A640 road Ⓒ.

Turn sharp left over a plank bridge across a stream and follow the Pennine Way, which winds across the upland moss for $\frac{3}{4}$ mile to the abrupt escarpment of Standedge. At a large stone marking the meeting of the Pennine and Oldham ways, go left along a broad path that curves above the rocky buttresses and pillars of the edge. The name Standedge probably derives from the Saxon word 'stan' meaning stone. From it there is a fine view across the gathering grounds of the River Tame, where many of the side valleys were dammed to power mills or provide water for the growing industrial towns. The grassy promontory overlooking the Castleshaw reservoirs immediately below was the site of a Roman fort.

Beyond the high point, marked by a triangulation pillar, the way gradually loses height. Crossing a couple of stiles, the Pennine Way then bears right at a fingerpost, dropping over a final stile onto a wide track, the Pennine Bridleway. Go left and then take the

The eastern portal of the Standedge Tunnel

second turning on the right to reach the main road opposite a small car park **D**.

The Pennine Way leaves the parking area to the left of the entrance by an information board, climbing above the road for a short distance before veering away through a gate onto the National Trust estate of Marsden Moor. A clear track runs ahead above the Redbrook Reservoir, shortly approaching an old stone boundary post above a boggy stream. Drop left to cross the stream, rising beyond to continue with the broad track. Passing through a gap in the low ridge ahead, the way eventually narrows, losing height to ford a brook at the head of Carr Clough before meeting the road below the flanks of Pule Hill **E**.

Cross to a lane opposite, Old Mount Road, but then bear off in a few paces

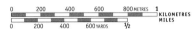

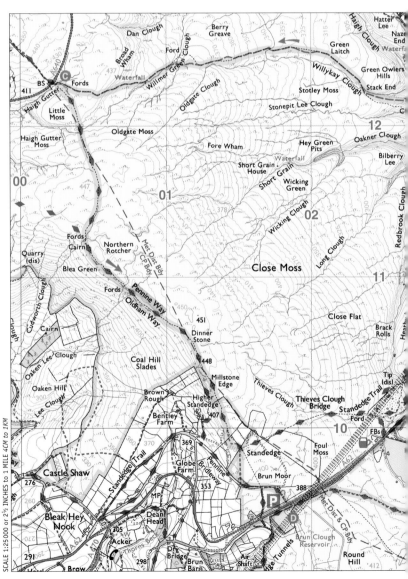

along a track to Hades Farm. After passing grassed heaps of quarry spoil, the track curves to a farmhouse. Follow the track ahead through a double gate and then swing right, descending to New Hey Farm. Where the track subsequently bends left into the yard proceed over a stile and, strike slightly right, walk downhill to a boundary. Ignoring a field-gate, go right and keep on beyond the corner to join a second wall.

Through a gate there, follow the left-hand wall to another farm, entering through an iron gate. Walk behind the house and ahead through gates to a field. The gully winding down the hill to a stile was part of the 18th-century coach road between Marsden and Manchester. A short drive then leads out to a lane. Go left to the main road, cross into Towngate and follow it around St Bartholomew's churchyard into Station Road, which leads you back to the car park. ●

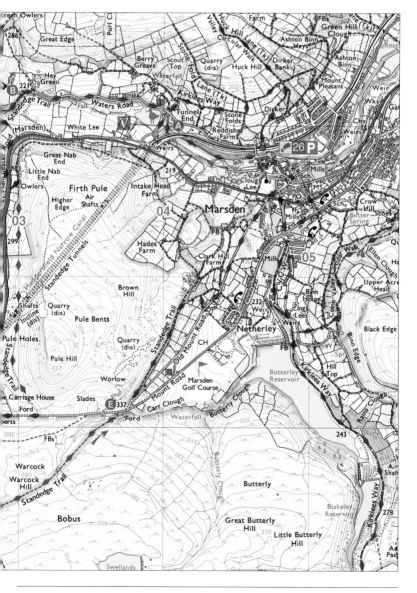

Derwent Edge

		GPS waypoints
Start	Fairholmes National Park Centre	🖉 SK 172 893
Distance	9 miles (14.5km)	Ⓐ SK 173 896
Height gain	1,600 feet (488m)	Ⓑ SK 170 919
Approximate time	4½ hours	Ⓒ SK 176 911
Parking	Car park at start – Pay and Display	Ⓓ SK 193 912
Route terrain	Clear moorland paths, *take care in mist*	Ⓔ SK 197 909
		Ⓕ SK 203 880
Ordnance Survey maps	Landranger 110 (Sheffield & Huddersfield), Explorer OL1 (The Peak District – Dark Peak area)	Ⓖ SK 187 884

From just below the massive wall of the Derwent Dam, the route hugs the shore of the Derwent Reservoir before climbing across fresh and bracing moorland to the prominent outcrop of Back Tor on Derwent Edge. There follows a superb scenic walk along the edge from where many of the best-known landmarks in the northern Peak District can be picked out, before descending to the Ladybower Reservoir. The forested slopes above the long tongues of water filling the Derwent Valley are a foil to the wild moors above and lend much charm to this striking landscape.

Towards the end of the 19th century, there was pressure to improve water supplies to the rapidly growing cities of Derby, Nottingham, Leicester and Sheffield. The upper Derwent Valley was an obvious choice for a vast reservoir, sparsely populated and relatively narrow, which facilitated the construction of the dam, and with a catchment that enjoyed (if that is the right word) a high annual rainfall. In time two more dams were built, forming a chain of reservoirs: Howden, Derwent and Ladybower, creating one of the largest man-made areas of water in Europe.

🖉 A path signed to the dam leaves the car park by the National Park Visitor Centre. Joining the lane, follow it right to sweep below the high wall. Because of the geographical similarities

between the Derwent Reservoir and the Möhne and Eder dams in the Ruhr, the RAF used the valley to practise for the famous Dambusters' raid in 1943, the subsequent film adopting the very same location. There is a memorial to those who lost their lives during the raid on the west side of the dam. Just beyond the bend, abandon the lane for a path that doubles back left Ⓐ. Sloping uphill through a conifer plantation, it passes the top of the dam wall to join a service track.

Follow it above the shore for almost 1½ miles towards the Howden Dam at the top end of the lake. As the trail then gently falls beside an embankment to the foot of Abbey Brook, look for a path signed off to Ewden via Broomhead for Bradfield and Strines Ⓑ. Almost

immediately, it swings sharp right to rise obliquely across the steep slope of Abbey Bank, leaving the plantation through a gate to continue beside a hollow way. After briefly turning more directly up the hill, carry on above a broken wall. Maintain your height where the wall subsequently falls away, walking on to a crossing of paths by a low cairn where Strines and Bradfield Gate Head is signed to the left **C**.

Higher up, the path curves to the right, following a broken wall, eventually reaching a stile beside a gate and signpost. Still making for Strines over a heathery moor, your immediate objective, Lost Lad is now clear ahead. Keep left at an unsigned fork, soon meeting a line of shooting butts below the end of the ridge. At that point turn right on a stepped path striking up beside an old ditch and embankment boundary, which briefly levels before a final assault on the summit of Lost Lad Ⓓ.

The prominent outcrop is named after a young shepherd boy who, beset by weather on the moor had become disoriented. As he lay on the hilltop dying from exposure, he carved the words 'lost lad' on a boulder. In good conditions, however, this is a grand spot and a topograph helps identify some of the features that can be seen. Carry on over the top, dipping before climbing once more to Back Tor on the ridge in front of you. To gain the summit trig point Ⓔ involves a scramble, but the view all around is something quite splendid.

The onward path curves to the right along the broad undulating spine of Derwent Edge, shortly passing a stone pillar that marks a crossing path to Bradfield Gate. Stick with the paved path along the edge, where the outcropping gritstone has been weathered into some weird and wonderful shapes. Encountered in slow succession are the 'Cakes of Bread', Dovestone Tor, the 'Salt Cellar', White Tor and finally the 'Wheel Stones', also known as the 'Coach and Horses'. Beyond there, the path gently loses height for another $\frac{1}{4}$ mile before reaching a junction of paths marked by a signpost Ⓕ.

Take the path right, marked to Derwent, which falls steadily to meet a lower path beside a wall. A little way to the right, it passes through a gate in the wall, further descending towards the right-hand corner of a forest plantation. Through another gate carry on at the edge of the trees, shortly entering the National Trust estate surrounding High House Farm. Continue down to a group of restored 17th-century barns, the path winding between them to leave through the smaller of the two gates. A paved way drops beside a pretty clough, curving away towards the bottom to end at a track Ⓖ.

Follow it to the right above the Ladybower Reservoir, soon reaching a bridge across Mill Brook. Beneath the waters of the reservoir at this point lies the submerged village of Derwent, which was drowned by the rising waters in 1943 when the dam was completed. Carry on along the lane for a further $1\frac{1}{4}$ miles, eventually passing beneath the Derwent dam to return to the car park. ●

Back Tor

Dovestone Edge

		GPS waypoints	
Start	Binn Green		
Distance	9¼ miles (14.9km)	� SE 017 043	
Height gain	1,750 feet (533m)	Ⓐ SE 019 045	
Approximate time	4½ hours	Ⓑ SE 037 049	
Parking	Car park beside A635, 1½ miles (2.4km) east of Greenfield	Ⓒ SE 031 044 Ⓓ SE 035 019	
Route terrain	A short scramble onto the upper moor, with faint paths along the edge, *take care in mist. Clear tracks around the lower reservoirs offer an alternative walk in poor weather*	Ⓔ SE 025 023 Ⓕ SE 018 031	
Ordnance Survey maps	Landranger 110 (Sheffield & Huddersfield), Explorer OL1 (The Peak District – Dark Peak area)		

An abrupt rocky escarpment defines the western perimeter of Dove Stone Moss overlooking the head of the Tame Valley. From below it presents a dramatic and forbiddingly steep slope, littered with ragged boulders arrested in unruly descent. Then, striding out along the rim, a parapet of shattered, weatherworn cliffs, a sequence of breathtaking views unfolds. The scrambling ascent of Birchen Clough can present a challenge when the stream is in spate, but once accomplished, the remainder of the route is not difficult.

� Beside an information board in the car park, a stepped path descends through conifers to a service track. The track drops to the western end of the Yeoman Hey Dam Ⓐ. Carry on above the bank of the lake, taking either branch where the track subsequently splits, since both lead to the higher dam of the Greenfield Reservoir.

The ongoing track continues into an ever-narrowing valley, the steep flank strewn with the debris from the crumbling escarpment above. Beyond the head of the lake, the track dogs the tumbling course of Greenfield Brook, crossing to its southern bank before rising to a turning area at the confluence of two higher ravines Ⓑ.

The route lies up that to the right, Birchen Clough, and involves fording the stream a couple of times, not always easy after heavy rain. Should you be defeated, you can rescue the day with a perambulation of the chain of lakes. Return to the foot of the Greenfield Reservoir and drop below the dam to pick up a rough path along the eastern shore of Yeoman Hey. Re-cross on its dam to point Ⓐ and go to the left, leaving the service road through a gate just a short way up on the left. The ongoing path runs above the shore of Dovestone and then swings across its much larger retaining dam. Continue around the southern shore past the sailing club to rejoin the main route at the foot of Chew Brook, point ⓕ.

To join the stream up Birchen Clough, skirt above the tunnel portal of the fenced aqueduct on the right. The 1,260-yard (1152m) tunnel bypasses the two upper reservoirs and was built to preserve water supplies to the mills lower down in the valley. With no obvious path, you must clamber over the boulders beside the stream, shortly switching to the other bank. Higher up as the gradient eases above a small cascade, re-cross to find a slanting path doubling back along the flank of the gorge.

Rising easily to the lip, it continues above the escarpment, revealing a distant panorama across the emptiness of the Saddleworth moors. The jagged rocks immediately below grab attention too, the most impressive being the Trinnacle, a detached three-pronged pillar of stone. Its ascent is reserved for experienced scramblers with a good head for heights and remember that getting up is not necessarily the hardest part of the exercise.

Carry on along the edge, revelling in the tremendous views opening along the valley as you round the headland above Ashway Rocks. A little farther on and set back to the left is the ornately carved Ashway Cross ⓒ. Now much battered by the elements, it is a memorial to James Platt who was killed in a shooting accident on the moors in 1857, shortly after his election as MP for Oldham.

Stride on above the narrowing clough of Ashway Gap, crossing its head and doubling back along the other side. The airy way runs on over Great Dove Stone Rocks, which tower over the reservoir and, on a good day, the temptation is to linger for the view. Maintain height above the long, climbing valley of Chew Brook, eventually swinging east across the moor to meet the northern end of the Chew Reservoir Dam ⓓ.

Located almost 1,600 feet (488m) above sea level, it was the highest reservoir in the country when it was built in 1912. Since 1971, the record has been held by the much larger but barely higher Cow Green Reservoir, which stands at the head of Teesdale.

Walk across the dam and turn down the service track into the valley, passing a small quarry, which provided stone for the project. One mile's walking brings you to a bridge at the foot of Charnel Clough ⓔ. Turn off immediately before it, dropping to a wooden footbridge across Chew Brook. The ongoing path follows the bed of a tramway along which more than 40,000 tonnes of clay was hauled up the valley to waterproof the dam. Before long the way dips to ford the stream out of Rams Clough, where the stone abutments of the trestle bridge that carried the track are still visible. Over a stile just beyond, fork off onto a lesser path, which falls through Chew Piece Plantation to meet the broad path encircling the Dovestone Reservoir ⓕ. To the right, it winds pleasantly back to the Yeoman Hey Dam. Cross and retrace your steps to the car park.

Towards the head of the Dovestone Reservoir, below the path, is the site of Ashway Gap House. It was an impressive Gothic-style hunting lodge, built by John Platt, elder brother of James whose memorial was passed on the ridge above. The family's money and prominent local standing derived from an engineering business founded by their father Henry, who began producing textile machinery at Dobcross in 1770. The business rapidly expanded and by the middle of the 19th century had become the largest such company in the world. The lodge was built in 1850 to host grouse shoots on the moor, but following the tragic death of James, John's passion for the sport evaporated and the house lapsed into

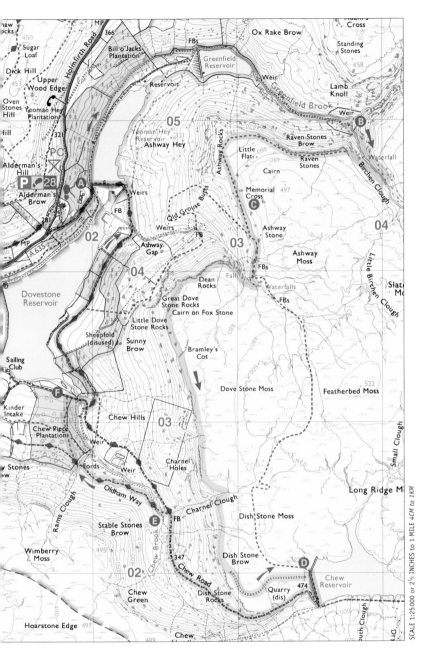

| 0 | 200 | 400 | 600 | 800 METRES | 1 |
| 0 | 200 | 400 | 600 YARDS | ½ | |

disuse. The valley estate was eventually acquired by the Ashton, Duckinfield and Stalybridge Waterworks in 1905, whose marker stones of ownership can still be seen on the hillside, and, for a time, the house was used for board meetings. During two World Wars it served as a hospital and subsequently a detention centre for Italian prisoners of war. It was finally demolished in 1981, and a levelling of ground, short flight of garden steps and clump of rhododendron bushes are all that is left now.

Further Information

Safety on the Hills

The hills, mountains and moorlands of Britain, though of modest height compared with those in many other countries, need to be treated with respect. Friendly and inviting in good weather, they can quickly be transformed into wet, misty, windswept and potentially dangerous areas of wilderness in bad weather. Even on an outwardly fine and settled summer day, conditions can rapidly deteriorate at high altitudes and, in winter, even more so.

Therefore it is advisable to always take both warm and waterproof clothing, sufficient nourishing food, a hot drink, first-aid kit, torch and whistle. Wear suitable footwear, such as strong walking-boots or shoes that give a good grip over rocky terrain and on slippery slopes. Try to obtain a local weather forecast and bear it in mind before you start. Do not be afraid to abandon your proposed route and return to your starting point in the event of a sudden and unexpected deterioration in the weather. Do not go alone and allow enough time to finish the walk well before nightfall.

Most of the walks described in this book do not venture into remote wilderness areas and will be safe to do, given due care and respect, at any time of year in all but the most unreasonable weather. Indeed, a crisp, fine winter day often provides perfect walking conditions, with firm ground underfoot and a clarity that is not possible to achieve in the other seasons of the year. A few walks, however, are suitable only for reasonably fit and experienced hill walkers able to use a compass and should definitely not be tackled by anyone else during the winter months or in bad weather, especially high winds and mist. These are indicated in the general description that precedes each of the walks.

Walkers and the Law

The Countryside and Rights of Way Act (CRoW Act 2000) extends the rights of access previously enjoyed by walkers in England and Wales. Implementation of these rights began on 19 September 2004. The Act amends existing legislation and for the first time provides access on foot to certain types of land – defined as mountain, moor, heath, down and registered common land.

Where You Can Go
Rights of Way
Prior to the introduction of the CRoW Act, walkers could only legally access the countryside along public rights of way. These are either 'footpaths' (for walkers only) or 'bridleways' (for walkers, riders on horseback and pedal cyclists). A third category called 'Byways open to all traffic' (BOATs), is used by motorised vehicles as well as those using non-mechanised transport. Mainly they are green lanes, farm and estate roads, although occasionally they will be found crossing mountainous area.

Rights of way are marked on Ordnance Survey maps. Look for the green broken lines on the Explorer maps, or the red dashed lines on Landranger maps.

The term 'right of way' means exactly what it says. It gives a right of passage over what, for the most part, is private land. Under pre-CRoW legislation walkers were required to keep to the line of the right of way and not stray onto land on either side. If you did inadvertently wander off the right of way, either because of faulty map reading or because the route was not clearly indicated on the ground, you were technically trespassing.

Local authorities have a legal obligation to ensure that rights of way are kept clear and free of obstruction, and are signposted where they leave metalled roads. The duty of local authorities to install signposts extends to the placing of signs along a path or way, but only where the authority considers it necessary to have a signpost or waymark to assist persons unfamiliar with the locality.

Countryside Access Charter

Your rights of way are:

- public footpaths – on foot only. Sometimes waymarked in yellow
- bridleways – on foot, horseback and pedal cycle. Sometimes waymarked in blue
- byways (usually old roads), most 'roads used as public paths' and, of course, public roads – all traffic has the right of way

Use maps, signs and waymarks to check rights of way. Ordnance Survey Explorer and Landranger maps show most public rights of way

On rights of way you can:

- take a pram, pushchair or wheelchair if practicable
- take a dog (on a lead or under close control)
- take a short route round an illegal obstruction or remove it sufficiently to get past

You have a right to go for recreation to:

- public parks and open spaces – on foot
- most commons near older towns and cities – on foot and sometimes on horseback
- private land where the owner has a formal agreement with the local authority

In addition you can use the following by local or established custom or consent, but ask for advice if you are unsure:

- many areas of open country, such as moorland, fell and coastal areas, especially those in the care of the National Trust, and some commons
- some woods and forests, especially those owned by the Forestry Commission
- country parks and picnic sites
- most beaches
- canal towpaths
- some private paths and tracks Consent sometimes extends to horse-riding and cycling

For your information:

- county councils and London boroughs maintain and record rights of way, and register commons
- obstructions, dangerous animals, harassment and misleading signs on rights of way are illegal and you should report them to the county council
- paths across fields can be ploughed, but must normally be reinstated within two weeks
- landowners can require you to leave land to which you have no right of access
- motor vehicles are normally permitted only on roads, byways and some 'roads used as public paths'

Further Information

The New Access Rights
Access Land

As well as being able to walk on existing rights of way, under the new legislation you now have access to large areas of open land. You can of course continue to use rights of way footpaths to cross this land, but the main difference is that you can now lawfully leave the path and wander at will, but only in areas designated as access land.

Where to Walk

Areas now covered by the new access rights – Access Land – are shown on Ordnance Survey Explorer maps bearing the access land symbol on the front cover.

'Access Land' is shown on Ordnance Survey maps by a light yellow tint surrounded by a pale orange border. New orange coloured 'i' symbols on the maps will show the location of permanent access information boards installed by the access authorities.

Restrictions

The right to walk on access land may lawfully be restricted by landowners. Landowners can, for any reason, restrict access for up to 28 days in any year. They cannot however close the land:

- on bank holidays;
- for more than four Saturdays and Sundays in a year;
- on any Saturday from 1 June to 11 August; or

- on any Sunday from 1 June to the end of September.

They have to provide local authorities with five working days' notice before the date of closure unless the land involved is an area of less than five hectares or the closure is for less than four hours. In these cases land-owners only need to provide two hours' notice.

Whatever restrictions are put into place on access land they have no effect on existing rights of way, and you can continue to walk on them.

Dogs

Dogs can be taken on access land, but must be kept on leads of two metres or less between 1 March and 31 July, and at all times where they are near livestock. In addition landowners may impose a ban on all dogs from fields where lambing takes place for up to six weeks in any year. Dogs may be banned from moorland used for grouse shooting and breeding for up to five years.

In the main, walkers following the routes in this book will continue to follow existing rights of way, but a knowledge and understanding of the law as it affects walkers, plus the ability to distinguish access land marked on the maps, will enable anyone who wishes to depart from paths that cross access land either to take a shortcut, to enjoy a view or to explore.

General Obstructions

Obstructions can sometimes cause a problem on a walk and the most common of these is where the path across a field has been ploughed over. It is legal for a farmer to plough up a path provided that it is restored within two weeks. This does not always happen and you are faced with the dilemma of following the line of the path, even if this means treading on crops, or walking round the edge of the field. Although the later course of action seems the most sensible, it does mean that you would be trespassing.

Other obstructions can vary from overhanging vegetation to wire fences across the path, locked gates or even a cattle feeder on the path.

Use common sense. If you can get round the obstruction without causing damage, do so. Otherwise only remove as much of the obstruction as is necessary to secure passage.

If the right of way is blocked and cannot be followed, there is a long-standing view that in such circumstances there is a right to deviate, but this cannot wholly be relied on. Although it is accepted in law that highways (and that includes rights of way) are for the public service, and if the usual track is impassable, it is for the general good that people should be entitled to pass into another line. However, this should not be taken as indicating a right to deviate whenever a way becomes impassable. If in doubt, retreat.

Report obstructions to the local authority and/or the Ramblers' Association.

 Useful Organisations

Campaign to Protect Rural England
128 Southwark Street,
London SE1 0SW
Tel. 020 7981 2800
www.cpre.org.uk

Camping and Caravanning Club
Greenfields House, Westwood Way,
Coventry CV4 8JH
Site bookings Tel. 0845 130 7633
www.campingandcaravanningclub.co.uk

Council for National Parks
6-7 Barnard Mews, London SW11 1QU
Tel. 020 7924 4077
www.cnp.org.uk

English Heritage
PO Box 569, Swindon, Wiltshire, SN2 2YP
Tel. 0870 333 1181
www.english-heritage.org.uk

Forestry Commission
Silvan House, 231 Corstorphine Road,
Edinburgh EH12 7AT
Tel 0131 334 0303
www.forestry.gov.uk

Friends of the Peak District
'The Stables', 22a Endcliffe Crescent,
Sheffield S10 3EF
Tel. 0114 266 5822
www.friendsofthepeak.org.uk

National Trust
Membership and general enquiries
PO Box 39, Warrington, WA5 7WD
Tel. 0844 800 1895
www.nationaltrust.org.uk
East Midlands Regional Office
Clumber Park Stableyard, Worksop,
Nottinghamshire S80 3BE
Tel. 01909 486411

Natural England
1 East Parade, Sheffield
S1 2ET
Tel. 0114 241 8920
www.naturalengland.org.uk

Ordnance Survey
Romsey Road, Southampton
SO16 4GU
Tel. 08456 05 05 05
www.ordnancesurvey.co.uk

Peak and Northern Footpaths Society
Taylor House, 23 Turncroft Lane,
Offerton, Stockport
SK1 4AB
Tel. 0161 480 3565
www.peakandnorthern.org.uk

Peak District National Park Authority
Aldern House, Baslow Road,
Bakewell, Derbyshire DE45 1AE
Tel. 01629 816200
www.peakdistrict.org

Peak District Information Centres
Bakewell
Old Market Hall, Bridge Street,
Bakewell, Derbyshire DE45 1DS
Tel. 01629 816558

Castleton
Buxton Road, Castleton, Hope Valley
S33 8WN
Tel. 01629 816572

The Moorland Centre, Edale
Fieldhead, Edale, Hope Valley S33 7ZA
Tel. 01443 670207

Upper Derwent
Fairholmes, Bamford, Hope Valley
S33 0AQ
Tel. 01433 650953

Ramblers' Association
2nd Floor, Camelford House,
87-90 Albert Embankment,
London SE1 7TW
Tel. 020 7339 8500
www.ramblers.org.uk

Visit Peak District & Derbyshire
Crescent View, Hall Bank, Buxton,
Derbyshire SK17 6EN
Tel. 0845 833 0970
www.visitpeakdistrict.com

Tourist information centres:
Ashbourne: Tel: 01335 343666
Bakewell: Tel: 01629 816558
Buxton: Tel: 01298 25106
Castleton: Tel: 01629 816558
Glossop: Tel: 01457 869176
Leek: Tel: 01538 483741
Manifold Valley: Tel: 01298 84679
Matlock: Tel: 01629 583388
Saddleworth: Tel: 01457 870336
The Moorland Centre: Tel: 01433 670207
Upper Derwent Valley: Tel: 01433 650953

Youth Hostels Association
Trevelyan House, Dimple Road,
Matlock, Derbyshire DE4 3YH
Tel. 01629 592600
www.yha.org.uk

 Ordnance Survey maps of the Peak District

The Peak District is covered by Ordnance Survey 1:50 000 scale (1¼ inches to 1 mile or 2cm to 1km) Landranger sheets 109, 110, 118 and 119. These all-purpose maps are packed with information to help you explore the area. Viewpoints, picnic sites, places of interest, caravan and camping sites are shown, as well as public rights of way information such as footpaths and bridleways.

To examine the Peak District in more detail, and especially if you are planning walks, Ordnance Survey Explorer maps at 1:25 000 (2½ inches to 1 mile or 4cm to 1km) scale are ideal.

OL1 – The Peak District (Dark Peak area)
OL24 – The Peak District (White Peak area)

OL21 – South Pennines

To get to the Peak District, use the Ordnance Survey OS Travel Map–Route Great Britain at 1:625 000 scale (1 inch to 10 miles or 4cm to 25km) or Road Map 4 (Northern England) at 1:250 000 scale (1 inch to 4 miles or 1cm to 2.5km).

Ordnance Survey maps and guides are available from most booksellers, stationers and newsagents.